CITIZENS OF HEAVEN

ISBN-13: 9781660222698

A Publication of Tall Pine Books
|| tallpinebooks.com

CITIZENS OF HEAVEN

A PARENT-CHILD GUIDE THROUGH LIFE'S BIG ISSUES

ALLISON MICHEL

Tall Pine

DEDICATION

This book is dedicated to my brother Dylan Barry, who loved me in a way that led me to the Father. Thank you for inspiring my walk with Jesus and waking my desire for Heaven when you went there. When we've been there 10,000 years, bright shining as the sun, we have no less days to sing God's praise, than when we first begun. See you real soon.

Thank you to my husband for providing for me to live and pursue my dreams. Rivers and Dylan, thank you for believing in me with childlike faith. You are living proof that God is a miracle working God.

For Zeke. May your life be filled with the abundance of Heaven as you walk with Jesus.

CONTENTS

USING THIS GUIDEBOOK

This is a simple and easy way to engage and connect with your child, small group or Sunday school class on important issues. This book is for preteen and teen boys and girls as early as age 10. Our kids are being exposed to many things covered in this book even earlier than that. This is also very much for the child or teenager that has already fallen into some of these traps. The heart of this book is to reach our kids before that happens and to guide you in developing a relationship with God.

There are a total of 14 chapters and the lessons build off each other. We start with an important foundation in the first 3 chapters, and then we discuss how our minds work and how habits and addictions form. We move into the much needed conversation about screen time and the tough topic of pornography. We talk about internet safety, social media and the importance of self worth, raging hormones and loving ourselves. There is a two part lesson on God's Design For Sex, where we discuss covenant and marriage with the second part covering how to deal with the hard topic of homosexuality and gender confusion.. We talk about the dangers of drug use and alcohol with real life scenarios of how easy it is to fall into the trap of addiction. The last 3 lessons are more specific to our relationship with God and who we are in Christ. Some of these topics covered are intense, and all need to be reviewed before being shared. All guidance in this book is based on scripture.

Each chapter consists of three parts:

1. Parent or leader introduction
2. The lesson
3. The discussion

As the parent or leader you simply read each part of the chapter while preparing. When you are ready to share with your child or group, feel free to teach the lesson or just read it. Some of you may choose to give it to your child to read on their own. Whatever works best for your family.

The discussion questions are designed to get conversation flowing as well as to guide you in prayer. I suggest leading by example in sharing your heart with your child or group so that they feel the freedom to respond and also to share. Take a minute in your preparation to think about what you may say. Some of these topics are sensitive and can be uncomfortable. I challenge you to push through any awkwardness and allow the discussion to generate heart-to-heart connection on the struggles they are facing or may face. Always ask if there are any questions and give a safe place for personal questions, comments or private prayer.

Everyone will need a journal or notebook to write in. This is for taking notes, journaling and writing prayers. It's great for the adults to participate in this!

Most lessons will take around 15-20 minutes to read. When doing discussion it is up to you how much time you want to put into it. If this is for your small group, I would allow at least 45 minutes for each chapter and discussion. Of course, each group will look different and you can modify the lessons in whatever way fits your needs.

While all of this is key information it is only scratching the surface of what needs to be ongoing conversations. I pray that you give input and expound on these topics during this study and after.

I pray this is a journey of getting to know the Lord in a new way that blesses you and brings transformation to your family or group. Let's go!

INTRODUCTION

When I was growing up, I needed to know this stuff. I always knew Jesus was real and at times I felt His presence and His hand on my life. When I walked down the aisle at my church at 14 years old, and gave my life to Him, I expected everything in and around me to change, and it didn't. I didn't know how to walk with God, or what that even meant. I had this deep need in my heart to belong and I searched for it in many wrong ways. I needed to hear the truth about the issues I was facing. I didn't hear it at home or at church. I walked away believing that I wasn't good enough and I bought into the lie that it was too hard to be accepted in the eyes of God. For a time, I took on this attitude of "do whatever you feel" and I let my feelings, emotions and desires lead my actions. I was on a path of destruction.

The price of not knowing God's love for me, left me riddled with guilt and shame. I battled feelings of worthlessness, and I struggled with a cycle of bad habits and I saw others in the depths of addiction. I thought there was no way out, so I dug deeper into darkness to run from everything, causing only more grief. This went on even into my 20's.

At 27 years old I faced the greatest challenge of my life when in a tragic car accident, I lost the one person that meant the most to me, my brother. I lost his wife too, and she was a best friend and a true sister to me. During my darkest day, I met the real and living God. One encounter with Him and the lies I had bought into were washed away. The pain and running turned into healing and peace. I saw my sin was not mine to pay for because of what Jesus did for me on the cross. I saw that it wasn't all about me, but about HIM. Beyond all, I found out that I BELONGED.

I became obsessed with heaven, because my brother and sister were there. I learned so many amazing things about it. God showed me that those of us who believe will all be there together soon, and this life is short. I learned I was wrong about Christianity. I thought being a Christian would be dull, boring and hard, but I have never been so alive and at peace in my life. I found out that it isn't about someday heaven, it is about heaven now. I found out, that we have access to everything in heaven and today my life is filled with meaning and purpose.

This guidebook is what I needed when I was growing up and what I believe a lot of us need now. My heart is to expose the traps the enemy sets, to talk about real issues the world throws at us and to counteract them with the powerful truth of God. This book is about seeing broken hearts belong, awakening people to life in Jesus and setting people on the path of their destiny. My prayer is to see a movement among families and youth that starts with a personal relationship with God, moves from friend to friend to change schools, communities and yes, cities.

One day, months after I lost my brother, I found this post card I never remembered seeing before he died. He had written it to me when he was on a trip in Costa Rica. At the right moment, it slipped out of a bunch of papers and onto the basement floor.

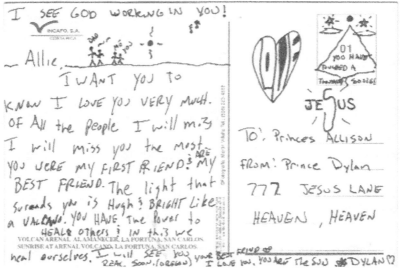

I got a postcard from my brother in heaven. He said the light that surrounds me is huge and bright like a volcano. I have a verse marked in my Passion Translation Bible, beside it I have written *ALLIE VOLCANO.*

Ephesians 2:19

My prayer for you is that every moment you will experience the measureless power of God made available to you through faith. Then your life will be an advertisement of this immense power as it works through you! This is the explosive and mighty resurrection power that was released when God raised Christ from the dead and exalted Him to the highest honor and supreme authority in the heavenly realm.

The resurrection power inside of you is wanting to wake up, and it is huge and bright.

Ephesians 2:10

We have become His poetry, a re-created people that will fulfill the destiny He has given each of us, for we are joined to Jesus, the Anointed One. Even before we were born, God planned in advance our destiny and the good works we would do to fulfill it!

God has a specific and amazing plan for your life. The enemy wants to get you off course by falling into the ways of the world, or by just going through the motions of religion. We are not only going to learn how to stay the course, but how to live life to the fullest and life abundantly.

As you journey through this guidebook this is my VOLCANO PRAYER for YOU!

Ephesians 3:16-17

I pray that He would pour out over you the unlimited riches of His glory and favor until supernatural strength floods your innermost being with His divine might and explosive power. Then by constantly using your faith, the life of Christ will be released deep inside you, and the resting place of His love will

become the very source and root of your life, providing you with
a secure foundation that grows and grows.

God Bless You,

Allie

1

WHY ARE WE HERE?

ETERNITY, FALLEN ANGELS AND LOVE

PARENTS AND LEADERS,

This foundational chapter gives a broad introduction of who God is. While you may know these truths, I pray you keep an open heart throughout all of these lessons and give God space to awaken you to new things in Him. We will build off of this as we go forward.

It is common for kids and adults to feel overwhelmed about the Bible or the topic of God. Let everyone see it's ok to not know everything, and we don't have to memorize the entire Bible. It is ok to not have answers to questions and to say so. Just reading and hearing the truth of God is planting seeds, and that is good!

Always give room for salvation for anyone in your family or group. If you would like, you may pray before each lesson and ask God to reveal Himself to each of you in new ways.

Don't forget, this is for you too!

I pray this first chapter stirs your hearts, minds and spirits, for more of the things of God!

WHY ARE WE HERE?
Eternity, Fallen Angels, and Love

Growing up I had the wrong idea about God. My family attended a great church. We dressed up most Sundays, and put out our best. We learned great Bible stories and verses and a formula for how to pray. We sang in the choir, had performances and did the hand bells. There were many good things about our church and in many ways it felt like home, but somehow, I missed the most important truths.

I didn't know that God, who created the stars and the sun and the moon, the great I AM, the all knowing all powerful, cared about *me*. I felt like there was a barrier between us, like He was too big, too far away and too holy, for little insignificant me. I believed that He was a big judge in the sky, solely focused on what I was or wasn't doing, and mostly on all of the things I did wrong. I thought He was watching and waiting for my next mistake, failure or sin. I had this longing in my heart for Him, but I didn't believe I measured up and the truth is, I didn't.

But I had it all wrong. You can know all of the Bible stories, all of the verses, all of the things about God, and not know *God*. You can go to church every week and walk away with nothing more than singing some good songs and some good information. You can be a *good* person, pray the right prayer, and go through the motions, but never access what God has readily available for you.

WHAT YOU BELIEVE ABOUT GOD WILL SHAPE YOUR LIFE.

It is important that you have the right idea of who God is, and it is even more important that you get to know Him.

Ecclesiastes 3:11
He has made everything beautiful in its time and He has set

ETERNITY in the hearts of man, yet they can't understand what God has done from beginning to end.

God is eternal. There was no beginning to God. He has always been and He will always be. It is very hard, if not impossible, to wrap your mind around that! We will forever and ever be learning who God is. Not just on earth, but in heaven.

Every single one of us has a desire for more than what is here on earth, because God put eternity in our hearts. We were created to find or bring eternal value, meaning and purpose to our lives, and the lives of others, starting now. The more we know God, the more we understand what He made us for. The more we know Him, the more we find who we are created to be.

GOD IS HOLY. He is pure, without darkness, perfect, sacred and divine. God is *all knowing* and *all powerful* and there is nothing greater than Him. I have heard it said that God is not only in heaven but heaven is actually in God. We do know He is on His throne in heaven, and Revelation 4 gives us a picture of that.

Part of it says, He has the appearance of jasper and ruby, and a rainbow that shines like an emerald encircles Him. There are flashes of lightning and thunder coming from the throne. In front of the throne there is a sea of glass, clear as crystal. There are living creatures there, they are covered with eyes, in front and in the back and they have wings. Day and night, night and day, they never stop saying, *Holy, Holy, Holy, is the Lord God Almighty, who was, and is, and is to come!*

This is amazing!

Many of us, when we think about heaven we just think about the clouds. Well there is a lot more to heaven! One thing God is not, is boring, and that is obvious if you just look around at all of creation, and then think about what heaven is like. Heaven is a real place, and it is beyond our wildest most incredible imagination.

Heaven is full of angels. God created this very beautiful angel named Lucifer. The Bible describes Lucifer as the highest of God's creatures. It says he was beautiful beyond description, a musician, given the highest position over all of the other angels and heavenly beings. At some point, God saw darkness, pride, or sin in him. You see, Lucifer wasn't satisfied with all he had, he wanted more. He wanted to take over heaven. He didn't want to do what he was created to do and just serve God, he wanted to BE God and he wanted to make his own rules and do it all his way.

God could have made the angels with no choice but to obey and serve Him. But they had a choice, and Lucifer chose to go against God, and so God cast him out of heaven to earth. Many other angels chose to follow Lucifer and abandon God. This is how the kingdom of darkness began.

There is a spiritual realm around us. One we can't see with our eyes but one that is very real. Angels and demons live there, and they are working for and against us. When we give our lives to God, we are His, but it doesn't mean we won't face some battles, some that are visible and some that are invisible. It doesn't mean the enemy can't take us off course.

God made the heavens and the earth. He has a master plan and there isn't one thing that happens that surprises Him. There isn't one thing He doesn't have all power and authority over. However, God did not make us robots. He gave us a free will to make our own choices. **God is building a Kingdom of ones who choose Him.**

IN THE GARDEN

Most of us know the story of creation. When God spoke, things *became*. When God said *light,* we got *day*. He made everything. When you imagine the vastness of the universe and space and all of the planets and stars and the sun, all the way down to the little animals and bugs. He thought it all up, and spoke, and it became. Then He made us.

And we know that He made us in His image. That means that we are a picture of God. That means that we are to be like Him. And the Bible says He made us in His image to rule. He told Adam and Eve, mankind or us, to subdue or conquer the earth.

So, Adam and Eve are in the garden of Eden. They are in charge. The garden sounds just like heaven, so beautiful and full of life. There was no sickness or death there. The animals got along and didn't kill and eat each other. I like to think maybe Adam and Eve could even talk to the animals. I mean, eventually she was talking to a snake right!

They were naked, yep, and didn't think anything of it! The best part, God was with them. He walked with them. He talked to them. We don't know exactly what that looked like, but we can imagine. They felt no separation from God. They were fully accepted, seen, loved and known by God.

Then the most terrible thing happened. Remember, Lucifer is on the earth. Satan, or Lucifer, came and he lied and tricked Eve and told her if she ate from the tree she wasn't supposed to eat from that she would NOT die. He also told her she would BE LIKE GOD. Eve believed him, and she went against God and ate from the tree and so did Adam.

Notice, Satan was tempting Eve with the very thing that got him kicked out of heaven. He was lying to Eve, telling her that if she did what he said, it would make her like God by knowing everything. Basically, He was telling Eve she didn't need to obey God, she could have it her way. This is the same temptation we face today, serving God, or serving ourselves.

Immediately, when Adam and Eve ate the fruit, their eyes were opened and they realized they were naked and they wanted to cover themselves. They felt ashamed or embarrassed, and they tried to hide.

This is when sin and death entered earth. To this very day, sin brings shame and yes, death.

While God knows the beginning, the middle and the end of our story, God did not design us for death. I believe that is why death is so hard for us to understand, because it doesn't make sense. God created us to live in union with Him and to live forever. But when sin entered the world, so did sickness, decay, and death.

I often hear of people blaming God for their sickness, or for losing a loved one. It is very clear that God is the ultimate power and authority over everything. While He can do anything He wants, and He can allow anything to happen, the reason we have suffering and darkness on the earth is because of Satan. Satan is here to steal, kill and destroy. God is the author of life.

Though we live in a world-system that is lead by the prince of darkness, Satan, those of us in Christ are set apart. God knew we couldn't do it on our own, we couldn't be perfect and follow all of the rules we were supposed to. He wanted us back. That is why He sent Jesus.

Jesus said, in this world we will have trouble, but because He overcame, we overcome. Jesus conquered sin and death when He lived a perfect life. He took on all the bad stuff we have ever done or ever will do. He took on sickness and death and He redeemed and restored us and He made us righteous in the eyes of God. **Righteousness** means, acting in accord with divine law, and being free from guilt or sin.

Those who believe in Jesus, those who follow and give their lives to Him, have full access to the throne of God. Jesus can relate to anything and everything we face, because he walked and lived on earth just like us. He has everything we need and He longs to provide for us. All we have to do is ask.

You know when I said I didn't think I measured up to God. Well, I was still seeing myself outside of Jesus, and I was still seeing myself as a lowly sinner. God sees us through Jesus, and through Jesus we measure up!

I no longer see God as far away. I no longer see Him as the *big bad rules God.* I no longer see Him focused on my sin, because He isn't. He sees me as His daughter.

GOD IS ABBA OR FATHER

On earth, I have two great dads. They love and care for me so much. They aren't perfect and they have even let me down from time to time, as all people in our lives may do. But I have gotten to know my heavenly Father. Most of the time, I call Him Papa or Daddy. He has never let me down and He is always there. I can boldly ask Him for anything at any time. I can call on Him and He will answer. I have learned, I don't have to go through this life trying to do things on my own. I don't even have to try to do everything right to earn my place with Him. Even when I fall or fail, He stays with me. He says there will be battles and tough times but as long as I am with Him, I will have the victory. I get to choose Him every day, and He chooses me simply because He loves me!

GOD IS LOVE

Love is the most powerful force in the world. God in His love is fighting for each and every one of us. He is your Holy, Eternal, Father and Creator. He loves you so much He allowed His Son to die in your place, even when you fail to keep all of the rules or you don't deserve it.

Jesus is the perfect picture of love, and the perfect picture of God. God sent Jesus, to cover you, to have your back, to comfort you, to relate to you, to talk to you, to walk with you, to protect you, and to die for you. The most amazing love beyond what we can understand. His love is stronger than anything the enemy could ever put in your path.

God does not want you going through this life being just like the world. It doesn't stop with believing in Him, that is the very beginning. Even Satan believes in God. Satan wants you to think being a believer is enough. If you stop there, you are allowing him to take away all of the power and authority God has put in you for this life. It doesn't stop with church or youth group or Sunday school, it is every day, always, and it is so good.

When you make Jesus the Lord of your life, you become His son or His daughter. This is *for real*. Just like your mom and dad or your grandparents love you, Jesus loves you a million times more. He cares about EVERY SINGLE THING in your life. Little things and big things. He also knows EVERY SINGLE THING about you. He even knows how many hairs are on your head!

When we are united with Jesus, all of the promises of His kingdom belong to us. That means, we have access to everything that He has in heaven. That's a big deal.

Following Jesus is not always easy, but He always provides everything you need.

Romans 8:19

The entire universe is standing on tiptoe, yearning to see the unveiling of God's glorious sons and daughters.

When you choose to be in the kingdom of God and make Jesus the Lord of your life, you are choosing love and you are choosing eternity. You are choosing the power that belongs to Jesus that now lives inside of you. You are choosing to partner with heaven and bring eternal purpose and meaning to your life and to this earth. You are choosing to join with Him and to conquer and rule with His authority and power on the earth. You are choosing to bring others into His kingdom and to do His will on earth as it is in heaven. He has missions and assignments for you to influence and change the world, and the world is waiting.

You are a very important part of God's story. While knowing about Him is great, knowing Him is where it is at!

Romans 8:38

So now I live with the confidence that there is nothing in the universe with the power to separate us from God's love. I'm convinced that His love will triumph over death, life's troubles, fallen angels, or dark rulers in the heavens. There is nothing in our present or future circumstances that can weaken His love.

DISCUSSION
PARENTS AND LEADERS

- Share what your thoughts or feelings were about God when you were growing up. Share your testimony with your child or have someone share their testimony with your group.
- Share some things you believed about God, that you have learned are not true.
- Share something new you heard in this lesson, or something you liked.

KIDS

- Share with your parents or leaders what your thoughts and feelings are about God. Don't worry about getting the right answer, but share what's in your heart.

FAMILY OR GROUP

- In your journal, write something about this first

chapter. It can be as short as a sentence, or as long as you would like.

PRAYER

Thank You God for who you are. Thank you for eternity. Thank you for setting it in our heart. Thank you for the gift of this life. Open our eyes to new and awesome things about you. Show us things about you we have never seen before. Help us to get to know you more! In Jesus name, Amen.

Be looking and believing to see new things.

2

LIVING WATER

THE INSIDE, THE OUTSIDE AND THE HOLY SPIRIT

PARENTS AND LEADERS,

There is a place deep inside all of us that longs to be connected with our Heavenly Father. One awesome way this happens is by the Holy Spirit. Just imagine, your kids growing in a personal relationship with Jesus and knowing the Holy Spirit. Often, Christians leave this part of God out. The Holy Spirit, the presence of God within us, is the key to walking with Him.

The Holy Spirit wants to be our best friend. This lesson will sow seeds of truth about the Holy Spirit and how we can rely on Him at any moment. I think our kids may get this better than us.

LIVING WATER

The Inside, the Outside and the Holy Spirit

One Sunday at church when I was 14 years old, while singing the hymn *I Surrender All,* I did just that. I let the tears flow, and in front of all of those seemingly perfect people, I got out of my seat and took the long walk to the front, all by myself. I was trembling, not for the choice I was making, but for the fear of not making it.

Something familiar that had been there all along, was calling me, drawing me to Himself, and it was God.

After that day, I knew when I died I would go to heaven. However, it seemed so odd to me that the world around me didn't change. Even at church everything was the same. I wanted everyone to feel whatever it was that I did, and I knew something had awakened inside of me that would never leave.

I wanted to be baptized but I really didn't know why. So, I was baptized. I remember trying hard not to cry again in front of everyone. I felt Jesus so close to me, and knowing what He did so that I could live forever with Him, moved my heart. But what really changed?

Life kept moving, it looked the same, I acted the same, though I knew things should be different. As time went on, I was making decisions that I knew were not pleasing to God. I felt guilty and started feeling really bad about myself. I would write in my journal, I am so sorry God, tomorrow I will not sin, I will not do bad things any more. The next day I would get up, try my hardest and fail all over again. It seemed like the more I tried to do what was right, the more I did wrong.

Romans 8:7-9

In fact, the mindset focused on the flesh (or ourselves) fights God's plan and refuses to submit to His direction, because it cannot! For no matter how hard they try, God finds no pleasure with those who are controlled by the flesh. But when the Spirit of Christ empowers your life, you are not dominated by the flesh but by the Spirit.

In my mind, God was far out of reach until I got my act together. The more I tried to do what was right in my own strength, the more I seemed to fail. My focus was *behaving to get to God,* but I just couldn't seem to get there.

You are not just a person with a body, you have a spirit within you. When you choose Jesus, your spirit joins with His and everything does change.

Romans 8:14

The mature children of God are only those who are moved by the impulses of the Holy Spirit. And you did not receive the "spirit of religious duty" leading you back into the fear of *never being good enough.* But you have received the "Spirit of Full Acceptance," enfolding you into the family of God. And you will never feel orphaned, for as He rises up within us, our spirits join Him saying the words of tender affection, "Beloved Father!" For the Holy Spirit makes God's fatherhood real to us as He whispers into our innermost being, "You are God's beloved child!"

This is everything. I was trying to do all of the right things and failed. **"Religious duty" is about what you do, not who you are.** As long as our belief about God accepting us is based on what we do, we will feel disconnected from our Heavenly Father, our Papa or perfect Daddy.

We will only be able to know *about* Him, and we will never have the true relationship with Him we were created to have. He can become real to us and we can know Him personally, by the Holy Spirit.

Check out this story from John 4, about Jesus before people knew that He was the Son of God, while He was still living on the earth. Pay attention, because this story has one of the most important keys to life.

GOD HAS GIVEN US AN ETERNAL GIFT, THE HOLY SPIRIT

One day when Jesus was very tired from a long journey He sat down on the edge of a well. This particular well was called Jacobs well. A woman came to get water out of the well. She was a

Samaritan woman, and back then Jews weren't supposed to talk to Samaritan women at all. They had strict laws that had to be followed and rules that should never be broken. But Jesus asked the woman to get Him a drink of water. She was shocked and said, "Why are you asking me for a drink of water, Jews won't even drink from a *cup I* have used!" Jesus told her "If only you knew who I am and if only you knew the gift God is wanting to give you, you would be asking me for a drink, and I would give you living water."

And she said, "but you don't even have a bucket, this is a deep well," and she asked him, "where do you find this living water?" And He said, "If you drink from Jacobs well you will be thirsty again and again and again, but if anyone drinks the living water I give them, they will never thirst again and will forever be satisfied. When you drink the water I give you it becomes a gushing fountain of the Holy Spirit, springing up and flooding you with endless life!

We know we need water for our bodies. If you go more than three days without water you can die. Water is vital to your body and it is important to give your body what it needs. Drinking water is something we do externally, or from the outside in.

Jesus is saying, He can give us water that is **living**. He calls it a gushing fountain springing up, or water that's coming from the **inside.** He is saying, if we drink His water we we will be satisfied. He called His water a fountain of the Holy Spirit and He said it floods you with endless life or eternity!

Just as we have to provide for our physical bodies, God has given us something for our spirit. When we unite ourselves with Jesus, He lives on the inside of us and He gives us the gift of the Holy Spirit. I love gifts, and I don't know about you but when the Creator of the world says He is giving you a gift, you can imagine it's the best gift ever!

So, let's talk about this awesome gift! The Holy Spirit is life giving and on the inside of us.

Jesus depended on the Holy Spirit to help Him in His life, and like Him, we can do that too.

THE HOLY SPIRIT, IS GOD'S VOICE INSIDE US.

God's voice comes in kindness and in peace. God's voice comes in gentleness. He comes to welcome you or to comfort you. He is always there. He never, ever, ever leaves.

The Holy Spirit will also warn you or convict you. If you are doing something that is harmful or not pleasing to God, in His loving way He will tug at your heart.

Sometimes, I can really feel the presence of the Holy Spirit, or hear His voice, and sometimes I can't, but either way I know He is there. The more I have gotten to know Him, the more I depend on Him. The more I listen for His voice, the more I know when He is speaking, or when it's my own thoughts.

Did you know the enemy will try and talk to you too? Yep. When he speaks he makes you feel anxious or scared. His voice is rooted in fear. He makes you feel like you have to do something or you are being pushed to do something. It's important we know the difference between voices.

THE HOLY SPIRIT IS YOUR INTERNAL BFF

You can have great friends but no one compares to the Holy Spirit. Being friends with the Holy Spirit means talking to Him and listening for Him to speak to your heart.

If you are feeling anxious, Holy Spirit can calm you, and comfort you, no matter what is happening. He can help you know what to do if you are in a difficult situation and He can give you strength. He can also help you help others, if you ask Him. He knows everything!

Holy Spirit loves you and just like God He is love. The Holy Spirit will never leave you.

Now let's go back to our story about the woman at the well. She had more questions for Jesus after He told her that He was living water. She was confused because it was unlike anything she had heard before. As she talked to Jesus, she saw that He knew everything about her. He knew about her sin, or the things she had done wrong, but He still talked with her and it must have been in the most loving, accepting way, because of what happened next.

She asked him questions about what was the proper or right way to worship.

This is important because it shows that once she met Jesus she wanted to do things right. This is a natural response when we decide we want to follow Jesus. This is how I felt when I said yes to following Jesus. I wanted to do the Christian thing right. But listen to what He said to her.

Jesus said to her, "from here on, worshipping the Father will not be a matter of the right place but with the right heart. For God is Spirit, and He longs to have sincere worshippers who worship and adore Him in the realm of the spirit and in truth."

He is saying, it isn't about doing it the right way, it is about engaging your heart with His. It's about opening your heart to Him and acknowledging He knows everything about you. He doesn't want you to focus on doing things right. He wants your heart.

This story is a great example of what happens when receive Jesus and allow Him to come alive to us. This is also a real illustration of how we will never be satisfied with just what is here on earth, or from the outside in. We were made for more. We are filled when we receive the living water from within. Filled to overflowing.

When we get the living water on the inside, we can't help but tell others around us! That is exactly what the woman at the well did, and then those people went on to tell others. **This is what we were made for.**

I know this is true because I tried to find satisfaction in many things the world had to offer and it didn't work. I looked for satisfaction in outside things. Things like having the coolest friends, wearing the best clothes or getting a lot of attention. Some things give a moment of satisfaction but then you need more. Like drinking water.

I remember the very moment the Living Water sprung up inside of me. It was the most profound moment of my life. For some, it is a slow and subtle shift in your heart. However, He did require something from me. He required me to *surrender all*. Not just in my head, but with my heart. When that happened, I felt so loved, accepted and full of life, that I wanted to stand on the rooftops and tell the world.

John 7:37

Some time after Jesus saw the woman at the well, He was at a very important feast. There was a crowd there and he stood and shouted out to the crowd "All you thirsty ones, come to me! Come to me and drink! Believe in me so that rivers of living water will burst out from within you; flowing from your innermost being.

This invitation stands. Jesus is calling you.

DISCUSSION
PARENTS AND LEADERS

- Share ways you have tried to be good enough for God.
- Share any area where you feel you have tried to find satisfaction in things that have not worked.
- Share how you hear from the Holy Spirit, or how you want to.
- Share why you love Jesus.
- Share something you believe Jesus loves about your

child or group. Be specific and speak to them individually.

KIDS

- Share or write ways you believe you hear from the Holy Spirit. It's ok if you don't know.
- Share if you learned something from the story about the woman at the well.
- Share and/or write in your journal something Jesus loves about you. If you can't think of anything, ask the Holy Spirit.
- Share something you feel Jesus loves about your parent or leader.

PRAYER

Thank you God for the gift of the Holy Spirit. Holy Spirit make yourself known to us and fill us with Your presence. Thank You for always being there for us. Thank You that you will never leave us and can always provide what we need. Help us to see You and know You in new and amazing ways. In Jesus name, Amen.

3

HIS BURDEN IS LIGHT

HEAVY LOADS, TRAPS AND REPENTANCE

PARENTS AND LEADERS,

Our Christian culture can be so focused on our "sinful nature" that we often miss the freedom that Jesus died to give us. When we are constantly told that we are sinners, I think it can disempower us to overcoming. This lesson teaches us to cast our cares on God and live in a way we are giving Him our burdens. It also teaches repentance as a way of life. These simple truths give us tools to walk with the Lord.

During discussion, without pressuring, reassure your kids that they can and should talk about their feelings and struggles. Model this for them so they know it is ok.

HIS BURDEN IS LIGHT
Heavy Loads, Traps and Repentance

My entire life changed when I let go of who I thought God was, and accepted His love for me. With all of my sins and failures, He chose me, and when I connected with His heart, it lead me to a true place of repentance. **Repentance is turning away from the things and beliefs God doesn't want in my life.** Repentance means changing from my ways to His ways, my thoughts to His thoughts.

As I have said, I was trying to get right in order to get to God. I thought if I could follow all of the rules I would have His approval. I was leaving out the most important part. Because of what Jesus did for me, I was accepted, just by believing. However, God loves us too much to leave us in our sin, and we need Him to help us grow and change to be like Jesus. **This is not a one time thing, this is a way of life.**

I also believed that being a Christian would be boring and would mean not having fun. I laugh at this now, because since I started walking with God, I have more fun than ever! God is the author of fun, laughter and joy. Therefore, you were made for all of those great things. Being in relationship with Him, is fun, and exciting and the best way to live!

Looking back, I see how the enemy got me off course. It wasn't like I wanted to wander down a dangerous path away from God, but that is what happened. Now that I see how sneaky the enemy can be, I want to blow his cover!

The truth is, no matter where you are or what you do, God is with you. However, the deeper you fall into sin, the harder and more difficult your life will be. God is able to change everything in a moment, but He wants you to walk with Him always, so that you never have to go through the pain and anguish sin opens you up to.

Psalm 31:4

As you guide me forth I'll be kept safe from the hidden snares of the enemy- the secret traps that lie before me- for you have become my rock of strength.

Sometimes we think of sin as obvious things. Like lying or cheating or stealing. While those things are clearly wrong, sin can be something that creeps into our lives. Even though we belong to God, the enemy or the world, wants to trip us up, change our course, and get us off track. This is why it is important for us to depend on God.

GETTING OFF COURSE

There were some things that went wrong in my life at a young age. Some of them were more obvious than others. One being, when my parents divorced. Others were subtle things, that maybe even no one besides me noticed. Either way those hurts were building up in my heart.

As I entered middle school, the pressures and challenges I was facing, grew and grew. At that point, friends were morphing into groups and cliques and I was trying to find where I fit.

Sometimes things happened at school that were hurtful or I faced stressful situations. I felt alone, and as I looked around, it seemed most everyone had it together but me, which wasn't true, but I believed it was.

1 **Peter 5:7**
Pour out all your worries and stress upon him *and leave them there*, for he always tenderly cares for you.

I had no idea that God had not intended for me to keep my worries and stress in my heart. No matter how big or small, God's desire is for us to cast our cares, anything and everything on Him. If it is important to you, it is important to Him. If you are feeling like you are alone, you must know, He is with you.

We were not made to carry anxiety and heavy burdens. The word burden means load. Stress and anxiety build in our lives when we believe everything rests on our shoulders, as opposed to trusting God.

The more hurt or pain you store in your heart, the heavier you feel and the harder it becomes to survive without some form of relief. When we live this way, all sorts of things break down. It is bad for us in every capacity. That is why God has given us a solution. That solution is to give it to Him and to leave it with Him.

TAKING ALL OF OUR STRUGGLES TO GOD IS PART OF WALKING WITH HIM

Not only does this relieve and lighten our hearts, it protects us from looking to something, someone or somewhere else to get freedom.

It is no coincidence that immediately after scripture tells us to give God our worries, it says this;

1 Peter 5:8
Be well balanced and always alert, because your enemy, the devil roams around incessantly, like a roaring lion looking for its prey to devour.

The enemy uses our weaknesses or insecurities to come into our lives. Here he is compared to a lion looking for its prey. Often lions choose the sick or injured as their prey. These animals have slower reaction times and may be isolated or alone. This is so telling!

Our Heavenly Father is saying if we are hurting, stressed or anxious, not paying attention and tending to our hearts, the enemy is waiting for any area he can trip us up.

That's just what happened in my life. I didn't know that I could give my problems to God, and find relief, I started believing things about myself, my future and my life that weren't true. I took the bait from the enemy and instead of taking God's way out, I took his.

If the enemy can get us down on ourselves, or use difficult circumstances we are facing to bring fear and anxiety, he may then tempt us with something to distract us from the heaviness. This is why we must be aware of things that are bothering us, hurting us, or insecurities we are feeling.

Hebrews 12:1

So we must let go of every wound that has pierced us and the sin we so easily fall into. Then we will be able to run life's marathon race with passion and determination, for the path has been already marked out for us.

God has gone before you and made a way for you through anything.

Today, when I am facing a challenging or difficult situation, or if my feelings get hurt, I know the first and best thing I can do is to take it to God and leave it with Him. When I lay it down, I am lighter and freer and I am able to stay the course He has marked for me.

An example of this would be; Let's say some friends at school are leaving you out or have disappointed you in some way. Whether they meant to or not, you feel hurt, and let down.

Whether you do it out loud in your room, or in your heart, you go to the Lord and you pray. You be still before Him and you know that He is with you. You rely on the Holy Spirit, your inside BFF, to comfort you. You remember who God is, His love for you and how He feels about you. In your heart, you hand over, or give Him the burden you are feeling. You tell him what happened, you tell him how you feel about it. You can even ask Him to remind you how He feels about you. You wait and you listen. He may speak to your heart. You may do this one time or ten times, but each time the fear, pain or problem you are facing rises, you can give it back to Him.

There are times I can feel the Holy Spirit comforting me so strong, that I would go through the hurt all over again because His presence is so good.

Worship always lightens our load. When we praise God in the midst of our problems, our problems don't seem as big. Setting our hearts on God, always brings healing and freedom.

It is also healthy, good and necessary to talk to people you can trust about your struggles. Ideally this would be your parents. You may be surprised at how they can help you, and if you can pray about these things together, that's even better. If you don't feel that is an option, ask the Lord who would be the right person for you.

If you are angry with someone, you will need to forgive them. Of course this doesn't mean what they did is right or ok, but it helps you to release that person, and the burden of being angry with them. Your heart wasn't meant to carry unforgiveness.

FOR EVERY PROBLEM YOU HAVE, GOD HAS AND IS THE SOLUTION

All of your problems won't go away, but your heart will be lighter. You may have questions, and concerns or need help making decisions about things going on in your life. God is inviting you to bring it all to Him. This is how you walk down the path that He has laid for you, letting Him lead and guide you in the right direction. This is how you learn to truly depend on Him.

When we hold things in, or allow our burdens to build, we are making ourselves vulnerable or open to the enemy. That is one way we can stumble and fall into temptation and sin creeps in.

GOD IS NOT LOOKING FOR YOU TO FALL, HE IS LOOKING TO LIFT YOU UP

If you do fall, if you do something you know in your heart was wrong, there is an easy answer. Take it to God. He already knows about it, He already paid the price for your mistake or your sin.

He is not mad at you because He loves you and forgives you. However, it is important that you work it out with Him.

GOD NEVER CHANGES HOW HE FEELS ABOUT YOU

God's love does not change. He loves you. Doing good things, doing bad things, He loves you.

The enemy wants to keep you in a place of condemning you for your sin and that is not Jesus. He wants to use the very thing he talked, tricked or tempted you into doing, to make you feel disconnected from God. He does it so you think you aren't worthy of God, but because of Jesus you are, and you need to know that and believe it.

No matter how bad or ugly you feel your sin is, God is not afraid of it, or ashamed of you. He will convict your heart when you are doing something wrong, but conviction and condemnation are not the same and it's important to know the difference.

- **Conviction** is when you feel bad or guilty about something you have done, or its the nudge in your heart that something you are doing is wrong.
- **Condemnation** says, you are what you have done wrong. Condemnation is when you take on the sin or guilt of your actions. Condemnation makes you want to hide and run from God, but that is the last thing you need to do. Jesus took on our sin, so we wouldn't have to. **Don't let the enemy get his way by hiding from God, run to God with your sin or mistakes, it makes the enemy so mad!**

Proverbs 28:13

If you cover up your sin, you will never do well. But if you confess your sins and forsake them, you will be kissed with mercy.

Again, anything you feel you need to hide from others, or more importantly from God, is the very thing you need to take to Him. One way the enemy gets a foothold into our hearts is by hiding. Just like in the garden when Adam and Eve sinned, they hid. Sin does not want to be exposed to the light! The light is the very thing you need to shine on any areas of darkness in your heart. God's light brings freedom! His light is covered in love, truth and grace.

God made a covering for Adam and Eve when they were ashamed and trying to hide. He wants you to know He has you covered, and He is waiting for you to invite Him into every area of your life.

IT'S GOD'S KINDNESS THAT LEADS YOU TO REPENTANCE

Romans 2:4
Haven't you experienced how kind and understanding he has been to you? Don't mistake his tolerance for acceptance. Do you realize that all the wealth of his extravagant kindness is meant to melt your heart and lead you into repentance?

God's love and kindness is beyond anything you can imagine. One touch from Him and you may be forever changed.

God loves us too much to leave us in our sin. God's grace is abundant and His mercy is new each and every day. He gives us a million chances. He is such a kind Father, always welcoming us into an encounter with Him which leads us into freedom.

We have all sinned, but we are no longer defined by our sin, we are defined by who we are in Jesus. We grow from glory to glory to look more like Him, to act and live like Him. Part of that is by seeking Him in all of our ways and repenting when He shows us a higher path. Repentance isn't always easy but it is simply awesome. Sin is a heavy burden to carry, so why not get rid of it!

Anxieties and burdens will weigh you down. Sin will steal your purpose, your joy and your hope. God will restore it.

IF YOU FEEL HOPELESS IN ANY AREA OF YOUR LIFE, THE ENEMY HAS SOLD YOU A LIE

For anyone who has something heavy on their hearts, God wants to make an exchange with you. He wants you to put Jesus in place of that burden.

Mathew 11:28-30 NIV

"Come to me, all you who are weary and heavy burdened, and I will give you rest. Take my yoke upon you and learn from me, for I am gentle and humble in heart, and you will find rest for your souls. For my yoke is easy and my burden is light.

Psalm 55:22

So here's what I've learned through it all: Leave all your cares and anxieties at the feet of the Lord, and measureless grace will strengthen you.

DISCUSSION
FAMILY OR GROUP

- Take some intentional quiet time to think and pray about burdens in your heart. Write in your journal anything that comes to mind. If you can't think of anything, simply ask God to reveal anything you are carrying that doesn't belong to you.
- Once you have written those down, release them to Him in prayer. Give Him space to fill your heart with truth in those places. You can write your prayer, pray with your group or family or do this on your own.
- Feel free to share if God is speaking to you in any way.

Share what He is replacing your burden with. This is how our trust in Him grows. If you don't come up with anything, try again another day. You can do this often.

- Now take some quiet time and ask God if there is anything you need to repent from. Feel free to write this in your journal. He may show you or speak to your heart now, or even later. Ask Him to shine His light in your family, or your heart, and expose things that don't belong or wrong beliefs about Him. If you think of anything or if He speaks to you, ask for His forgiveness. One time is enough! Trust and believe in His forgiveness for you. Make sure you leave it with Him!

This can become a regular practice in your life and will help you to live lighter and freer. Freedom is awesome!

Pick someone to read this message for your life.

Psalm 32

How happy and fulfilled are those whose rebellion has been forgiven, those whose sins are covered by blood.

How blessed and relieved are those who have confessed their corruption to God! For he wipes their slate clean and removes hypocrisy from their hearts.

Before I confessed my sins, I kept it all inside; my dishonesty devastated my inner life, causing my life to be filled with frustration, irrepressible anguish, and misery.

The pain never let up, for your hand of conviction was heavy on my heart. My strength was sapped, my inner life dried up like a spiritual drought within my soul.

Then I finally admitted to you all my sins, refusing to hide them any longer.

I said, "My life-giving God, I will openly acknowledge my evil actions"

And you forgave me!

All at once the guilt of my sin washed away and all my pain disappeared!

This is what I've learned through it all: All believers should confess their sins to God; do it every time God has uncovered you in the time of exposing. For if you do this, when sudden storms of life overwhelm, you'll be kept safe.

Lord, you are my secret hiding place, protecting me from these troubles, surrounding me with songs of gladness! Your joyous shouts of rescue release my breakthrough.

I hear the Lord saying, " I will stay close to you, instructing and guiding you along the pathway for your life. I will advise you and lead you along the way and lead you forth with my eyes as your guide. So don't make it difficult; don't be stubborn when I take you where you've not been before. Don't make me tug and pull you along. Just come with me!"

So, my conclusion is this: Many are the sorrows and frustrations of those who don't come clean with God. But when you trust in the Lord for forgiveness, his wrap-around love will surround you.

So celebrate the goodness of God! He shows this kindness to everyone who is his. Go ahead -shout for joy, all you upright ones who want to please him!

PRAYER

Thank You Father for Jesus. Thank You that He died so we could be set free. Thank You for Your love and kindness towards us, even when we are in darkness. Thank You for inviting us into a life of goodness with You. Shine your light on our hearts and our families so that we can grow to become more like You. Open our eyes to areas where we don't know You or have wrong beliefs about who You are and Your love for us. Help us to live a life of repentance to lead us away from things that harm us, and towards You. In Jesus name, Amen.

4

YOUR MIND IS A GATE

HABITS, ADDICTION AND A RENEWED MIND

PARENTS AND LEADERS,

Understanding how habits and addictions form in our lives is important. Teenagers can be impulsive, and experimental during their developmental years. They will be faced with choices where they will be confronted with many things that can lead to addiction. No one ever sets out to be an addict, yet millions upon millions of people are. No one ever thinks it will be their child.

As a parent, one of my biggest fears for our children is that they would find themselves battling addiction. I have seen too many people lose their purpose and even their lives, just trying to get free. I believe if we simply educate them on how addiction works and teach them how to be vigilant and guarded we are a step ahead. More importantly, if we can equip them with the tools to make wise and strong choices, they may never go down that path of struggle. This is such a broad topic, please add whatever the Lord leads you to. Too often we want to protect our children from the harsh truths of the world so we don't say hard things, but if we talk to them about things we have learned, struggled with or seen, it will help shed light on the truth and they will be more prepared. We can educate them now or we can let the world do it.

This chapter discusses the pathways in our mind and how we empower what we focus on. This lesson lightly touches on how addiction works, and how to guard ourselves from it. Later, we will dive deeper into the topics of drugs and alcohol.

Your Mind is a Gate
Habits, Addiction and a Renewed Mind

There have been many times, I have allowed the enemy's voice to be louder than my Heavenly Father's, and it has gotten me in trouble. Forgetting who God is, who we are in Him, and His love for us, is one way the enemy gains access to our hearts. So, I want to set the record straight.

There are many things the world wants to tell you are ok, or even good, that are not! We are going to learn what God says about some of these things and why He says it. I can already tell you the answer, it's because He loves you. His ways are higher than ours, or the ways of the world, and He has great things in store for you as you follow Him. We are going to learn how to be empowered in the midst of hard choices and how to overcome the traps the enemy has set for you. There is a battle going on, and the enemy wants to get you off course.

One thing you should know about this battle is *it starts in our minds.* Your mind or your brain is obviously the place that tells your entire body what to do. Your brain isn't fully matured or done growing until you are about 25. That is why little kids can't drive cars or vote or do a lot of things like that because their brain doesn't have the understanding like adults do. You may think you know everything but guess what, you don't!

Side-note, there is no age limit on the Holy Spirit. In fact, children are often more open to hearing from the Holy Spirit than adults! So, you are never limited in your relationship with God just because of your age, or if you have a learning disability. Maybe you have a special need or you have been diagnosed with ADD or ADHD. Maybe you have something you believe has made life more difficult for you. Well, if that is you, there is something important you need to know. God is much bigger than anything on earth that may make things challenging for you. He will show up bigger for you in any area you need Him to! I have learned that areas where I am weak, are the exact places that I see God most! He has a way of taking our disadvantages and making up for them.

There is much to know about how God designed our brains and how they develop or grow and change. One thing I have learned about is something called **neural pathways**. There are pathways in your brain that send information or tell your body what to do. Think of these pathways like trails through a forest.

WHAT YOU FOCUS ON YOU EMPOWER

Your brain is full of trails, or thoughts or messages. The more you focus on something or the more often you think about something, it's like going down that same trail. For example, let's pretend your favorite thing to think about is cake. Every time you think about cake your mind is walking down that one trail in your brain. Let's say you think about cake a whole lot, that trail gets deeper and bigger. After some time, you won't even try to think about cake but your mind automatically goes there.

Have you ever had a song get stuck in your head? You don't want to think about it, but it keeps coming up. That catchy song has made a trail in your mind and sometimes your brain is automatically sending you down that thought path. Sometimes it can be difficult to stop thinking that song even when you want to.

The more you are thinking about, looking at, focusing on

something, the bigger it will become to you. The more space in your mind something is taking up, the more it can become a habit. This is important to understand because this can lead to good things or bad things.

If one of my kids gets sick with a stomach bug, and I start thinking I am going to get it, the more I think about it, the more I start to believe it. Before I know it, I may actually start feeling stomach pains or like I am going to be sick. The point is, our mind is powerful, and we have to be careful what we are focusing on.

I have a family member going through some hard health stuff. It is scary not knowing what the future looks like for him. When the doctors told us some of the things he may have, I immediately started Googling them. The more I read about how bad all of these things could be, the more I started to be afraid, and feel discouraged. I had to make a choice to stop letting my mind go there.

I remembered how much God loves Him, and how God knows everything and has all the answers. I started focusing on the promises God has for his life and I even went a step further and chose to focus on what is in heaven and not what is on earth. On earth he may receive a diagnosis that looks like it could be a struggle, but God is a healer. He is more powerful than any disease or diagnosis. While we see the real facts that he may be sick, and we are thankful for doctors and medicine, we have to keep our eyes on heaven where there is no sickness. I have to choose to believe what God's will is over all of the what if's and what could be's. As I do that, I have peace and trust, instead of stress and anxiety.

WHAT YOU PUT IN, IS WHAT YOU WILL WANT

The more you focus on something, the more you will want

that thing. I notice, the more I am scrolling on my phone, the more I want to. Even if I'm looking at the same stuff over and over. Before I know it, I'm grabbing my phone to scroll without intentionally doing so. This concept is true for everything.

Proverbs 4:23

So above all, guard the affections of your heart, for they affect all that you are. Pay attention to the welfare of your innermost being, for from there flows the wellspring of life.

Your mind is like a gate. It is the gate to your heart. The gate to your soul. We must protect what goes in our mind-gate. We have a choice what we look at our what we watch on TV. We have a choice what games we play and what pictures we look at on the internet. We need to pay attention to what we are putting in. Not just as kids, but as adults. God says the source of our life, or the issues of our life flow through our heart. You may not see it at first, but what we look at, listen to, or allow into our hearts, will affect our entire lives. I know this to be true!

Just because you think or see something inappropriate or wrong doesn't make you bad! However, the danger is when you keep looking at or thinking things that aren't good for you, **your brain can make a path to that thought and you can start thinking of it, even when you don't want to.** This is one sneaky way the enemy wants to get to you.

The truth is, the more you intentionally seek to look at, listen to and think about good things, the more you will pursue those good things.

ADDICTION

An **addiction** is a when you have a habit in your life that you feel compelled to do. The word addiction means **enslaved by or**

bound to. An addiction is when you feel something has control of you. Addictions can come in many forms. People can be addicted to things they look at or things they think about. People can be addicted to shopping or coffee or food or alcohol or drugs.

NO ONE EVER THINKS THEY ARE GOING TO GET ADDICTED TO SOMETHING, YET MILLIONS OF PEOPLE ARE STRUGGLING WITH ADDICTION

PEOPLE EVERYWHERE ARE STRUGGLING TO STOP DOING SOMETHING THEY FEEL LIKE THEY CAN'T STOP DOING. I personally know people that have been trying to stop the thing they are addicted to for 20 years.

Why can't they stop doing something if they want to? That seems crazy right?! I believe, if you understand how this works, and you understand that **God has equipped you to overcome the temptations that can lead to addiction,** you will not struggle with something that God never wants for your life.

Let's look at one way addiction happens. God designed our brains with a **reward system** so that we would survive. He created our brains to reward us when we do good things like eating and drinking. For example, when you get hungry, you eat. You may not know it, but your brain releases something called **dopamine.** Dopamine creates **a pleasing or good sensation or feeling.** We were designed this way so that we would take care of our bodies and do the things we need to do for survival.

When you complete your work at school, finish a task or win a race, you may get a surge of dopamine. Dopamine is a natural and good thing God gave us to **motivate** us or to send a signal to our minds to **DO THAT AGAIN.**

The dangerous thing about dopamine, is what the enemy has done with it. The enemy wants to take this good thing God has given you, to get you addicted to that rewarding feeling. The enemy wants to take this natural process in your brain, and get you to abuse it by becoming addicted to something. You can become addicted to anything.

The following is an example of what happens with a person who becomes addicted to drugs.

Let's say when you eat an apple your body gives you 1 shot of dopamine. When you eat cake you get 2 shots of dopamine. We know that apples are healthier than cake, but rarely do we crave apples! Of course it is ok to eat cake, but we know that we can't have it for every meal. Eating cake gives us a little extra release of dopamine, so we may crave cake again. Sometimes we don't even consciously know it but we are craving sugar. This is a result of our brains release of dopamine when we ate the cake, but overall this is something most of us are able to manage. Especially as your brain matures and you get older.

When you take an illegal drug you may get 10 shots of dopamine all at once. Certain drugs are intentionally created to make dopamine release in an unnatural way. At first, taking that drug may give you a strong or even rewarding feeling, though it may be harmful to other parts of your body, specifically to your brain. After your brain releases that high amount of dopamine your brain is now sending you a very strong, stronger than ever signal, to do that again! Even if you know it's wrong, or that you shouldn't do it, you have a nagging feeling to do it again.

It would be like someone tapping on the back of your shoulder constantly. Tap, tap, tap, tap, and they won't stop. The only thing that can get that tapping or that craving to stop, would be to do that drug again.

So let's say you do that exact same drug in the same way again. Last time you got 10 shots of dopamine. The 2nd time you only get 9. Your brain is now telling you, that's not enough, you need more. So, you have to do more of the drug to get back to 10. The problem is, the more you do the more you need and you never feel satisfied because the craving doesn't go away. This is an example of the vicious cycle of addiction.

There are many things other than drugs that you can become addicted to that can be just as compelling as the example. Later we will address some of those things deeper. However, it is important that you recognize the enemy wants to trip you up where you are weak, and it can all start in your thought life. That is why we must protect our minds and our hearts. If we stay guarded, and choose to pursue good things, it's harder for bad habits and addictions to come in.

Philippians 4:8
So keep your thoughts continually fixed on all that is authentic and real, honorable and admirable, beautiful and respectful, pure and holy, merciful and kind. And fasten your thoughts on every glorious work of God praising him always.

The more you practice this, the more it becomes natural and easy for you. The things God is describing here are things that bring love, life and freedom. He has given you built-in discernment to know what these things are. The Holy Spirit will guide you in this and if you are wandering down a path of thoughts that aren't good for you, He will guide you back if you ask Him. It is important that we FIX, SET, or FASTEN our minds on these things. That means intentionally focusing on good things, not just daily but always.

Have you ever been around someone that always complains. Like they can find something wrong with anything so they find something negative to say about everything and everyone. This person's mind is set on what is wrong. What about looking for what is right? Looking for the good, or the beauty in things or others. When you look for God in anything you will find Him. Now that is a good habit to have!

Romans 12:2 NIV

Do not conform to the pattern of this world, but be transformed by the renewing of your mind.

Did you know you can actually renew your mind, and by doing so you will be transformed or changed to become more and more like Jesus? Yes! That is one big reason you are on earth and what you were created to do. And If you are struggling with your mind, God is so good that He gives us a brand new day every day to start over fresh and new. One way you can renew your mind is by getting into what He says. I get renewed by reading my Bible and being reminded of all of His promises for me. I get renewed in worship and prayer. It is a part of my regular life. If I don't, I start to conform to this world and be just like any old person. God has such a better life for me and for you.

WHEN MY MIND IS RENEWED I AM CREATING NEW AND GLORIOUS PATHWAYS IN MY BRAIN

Renewed pathways build me up, encourage me, empower me and equip me so that in any situation I am prepared. When my mind is renewed, any battle is easier because I know who I am and whose I am and the enemy can't easily trick me. When my mind is renewed, I not only am the best version of myself but that overflows to others.

Simply reading God's word, praying, engaging with Him, helps keep our mind renewed. Just acknowledging Him in all we do. Throughout my day, I talk to Him. About anything and everything. Sometimes out loud, sometimes in my heart, but keeping my heart postured that He is there, makes everything better.

SETTING YOUR MIND ON HEAVEN

Colossians 3:2 NIV

Set your mind on things above, not on earthly things.

We live in this world where we are exposed to a lot of stuff we don't want to be and where we face difficult situations, but the point is, we can focus on having a heavenly mindset. Maybe this sounds impossible to you, but this is instruction straight from your Heavenly Father who knows all things. With Him, it's possible.

Heaven is full of the glory of God. Full of hope, love, peace and joy. Heaven has more than everything you could need or imagine, and we have full access to it because of Jesus.

Even on my hardest days when everything seems to be falling apart, If I set my heart, my thoughts, on the One who is in heaven, everything changes. For every problem you could have, heaven has a solution.

When I feel like no one likes me, God shows me I'm loved. When I am hurt, He provides comfort. When I feel discouraged or depressed, He fills me with hope. When I feel insecure or unworthy, He lifts me up. When I am sad, He will fill me with joy. If I feel alone, He shows me He is there. Whatever is happening, we can train our minds to see things from the perspective of heaven.

If we only focus on earthly things, or the problems we are facing, we can quickly become discouraged. The rewards that the world offers in the form of habits or addictions leave you hurting and unfulfilled. We can take anything or any thought and submit it to heaven and quickly it can be filled with hope, and excitement for the future. That's simply how God's Kingdom works!

God designed you with a reward system in your brain to give you good feelings when you choose or think good things. It is a great thing when we treat ourselves the way we were made to. When we practice healthy habits and don't abuse the system we will protect ourselves from all sorts of problems and struggles. Simply making good choices by what we allow in our mind, by what we listen to or put into our bodies will protect our hearts and our future.

2 Corinthians 4:17-18

We view our slight, short-lived troubles in the light of eternity. We see our difficulties as the substance that produces for us an eternal weight of glory far beyond all comparison, because we don't focus our attention on what is seen but on what is unseen. For what is seen is temporary, but the unseen realm is eternal.

DISCUSSION
PARENTS AND LEADERS

- Share some good things you focus on that bring life and light to your day.
- Share a story about someone you know who has struggled with habits or addiction.
- Share a habit you would like to change.

KIDS

- Share something you don't like to see on TV or online.
- Share or write down some thoughts you have that you don't like.
- Now share or write what you think the Holy Spirit is saying instead.

PRAYER

Thank You Father for that you have given us the mind of Christ. Shine Your light on our minds and wash away any pathways that are not in line with the truth. Expose areas where we are weak so that

You can be strong for us. Protect us from things that can cause bad habits and addiction and convict us by Your Spirit when we are in danger. Activate our thoughts to be heavenly thoughts and create a deep desire in us to fill our hearts and minds with You. In Jesus name, Amen.

5

CYBERSPACE

SCREEN TIME, PORNOGRAPHY AND PROTECTING YOURSELF

PARENTS AND LEADERS,

This next chapter discusses how too much screen time can affect our minds. It also talks about the most dangerous thing on the internet, Pornography. Parenting today is more complex than ever due to the internet. Our children are facing all sorts of things at extremely young ages that can be life altering. Navigating this territory is new and challenging. Knowing when to get cellphones, what limits to put on internet use and how to manage it all, can be overwhelming. While there are resources to help guide us, one thing is for sure, communication is key. This next lesson will assist you in connecting with your children or group on these difficult topics that they will face, if they haven't already. As long as your child or group has had the talk about sex, this is appropriate and important for them to hear.

I read a book titled, *Disconnected*, by Thomas Kersting. He is a renowned psychotherapist, author, TV personality, as well as a high school counselor for many years. Around 2009, he noticed an inordinate amount of teens being diagnosed with ADD and ADHD, where in the past most children were diagnosed at a much younger age. He started to research how the human brain works and how it responds to screen time. His research showed that as little as three hours a day of stimulating activity or "screen time" in a developing brain can literally rewire it.

This re-wired brain is great at posts, snaps, likes and video games, but struggles to make eye contact with another person. His research talks about how if some parts of the brain like *social skills* aren't used, your brain can prune or discard those to the point a person is almost incapable of being able to socialize or engage. I have seen what I believe is a result of this in real life. Teens are using their phones as a crutch in every way instead of being forced to deal with reality.

In his book, Kersting, talks about how in his counseling not a day goes by that he doesn't see a high school student having an emotional breakdown over something very trivial. He shares a story of how a child even wrote a suicide note due to being grounded from their phone for one night. He traces many problems of anxiety, depression and even mental illness, to **screen addiction**. In January of 2019, sisters age 12 and 14, killed their mother and it is believed to be in retaliation because she took their cell phones from them. I have heard numerous stories of suicide and even murder related to teens losing their cell phones, all because they were severely addicted to them.

He also shares the amount of kids that are now on medication due to being unable to focus. He explains what happens in the brain when you are constantly switching tasks online and how it interrupts the natural flow of thought. Because tweets, posts, texts and the like are all done in short, quick bursts, over time the brain becomes accustomed to this form of communication making it harder to have longer thought patterns. As a result, kids are being prescribed "focus medicine" at alarming rates, and many are abusing them.

Not only are kids addicted to being online, but the even greater threat is what they are becoming addicted to. Unfortunately, these days our children are exposed to pornography as early as 7 years old, and it is way more graphic than ever before. They all have access to it if they are able to get online. We truly need to educate them and equip them to make wise choices.

I am a member of a closed group on Facebook where parents ask questions about how to deal with issues regarding technology. Many of the questions are about how to use certain safeguards and monitoring apps, how to use filters, set time limits and all of the things we want to do as parents to protect our kids online. I see comments daily about how kids have found a way around the safeguards, time limits and filters. Many of the questions I have seen, are parents who have found out the hard way about their child or teens inappropriate online behavior. So many kids are looking at porn, despite what their parents have done to try and protect them.

All families are different, all kids are different, and we have unique styles of parenting when it comes to how we manage our family online. But one thing is for certain, we have got to wake up and they need to hear from us.

Statistics vary but are astounding. Research from enough.org regarding our youth and porn reveals the use of filters by parents has not worked. The words "sex" and "porn" rank fourth and sixth among the top ten most popular search terms.

The average age of first time exposure to pornography is 11 years old. Research suggests that children under the age of 10 account for 1 in 10 visiting pornographic video websites. Obviously this exposure is impacting the sexual development in children and is responsible for dangerous sexual behavior. Kids are using porn to teach them about sex. Children and teens are at a high risk of developing an addiction to porn specifically because their brains are still developing. Many teens surveyed said they tried to stop watching porn but could not.

The following Statistics are from Covenant Eyes. Covenant Eyes is a great resource for anyone dealing with pornography.

- 28,258 users are watching porn every second.
- $3,075.64 is spent on porn every second
- 88% of scenes in porn films contain acts of physical aggression and 49% of scenes contain verbal aggression.
- **1 in 5 mobile searches are for pornography**
- 90% of teens and 96% of young adults are either encouraging, accepting, or neutral when they talk about porn with their friends.
- Just 55% of adults 25 and older believe porn is wrong.
- Teens and young adults 13-24 believe that *not recycling* is worse than viewing pornography.
- 1 in 5 youth pastors and 1 in 7 senior pastors use porn on a regular basis and are currently struggling. That's more than 50,000 church leaders.
- 43% of senior pastors and youth pastors say they have struggled with pornography in the past.
- 64% of Christian men and 15% of Christian women say they watch porn at least once a month.
- Only 7% of pastors report their church has a ministry program for those struggling with porn.

For some of you this has been on your radar, you may have dealt with this issue in your family or marriage. The enemy is destroying what sex is about in the minds of so many who are looking at porn. He is baiting our children who are just one click away from life altering images and getting them hooked on something they don't understand. This lesson will guide you and your child or group into a discussion that needs to happen. While it may be awkward or uncomfortable for you, kids and teens need to hear this! If they already know what pornography is, this will reinforce what they need to know. This is just scratching the surface of this topic but is very impactful. We will get into more online issues in following chapters.

After the lesson, set the tone that there is no shame in discussion. Emphasize that no one is in trouble if they have been exposed or are struggling with pornography. Let conversation flow about inappropriate pictures online. Most kids have seen things they know are wrong and they may want to share. Even the most intentional and involved parents find out their kids have been exposed to pornography. Try not to react in shock or fear if you discover they have. They need to know it is safe to talk either now or in the future. It can be devastating to find out if it is your son or daughter, but finding out now, is better than later. Beyond this discussion and prayer, there are resources available about next steps to take.

Cyberspace
Screen Time, Pornography and Protecting Yourself

When I was growing up, if we wanted information about something we had to go to a library and read or check out books or encyclopedias. Now we can type a question or even ask Siri or Alexa and get answers immediately. It's incredible! The internet can be great for many reasons and extremely helpful. However, there is a lot you should know about being online to keep yourself safe.

In our last lesson, we talked a little about how our minds work. We went over how there is a battle going on, and one place the battle is, is in our thoughts. We lay good pathways of thought when we focus on heavenly things or good and healthy things. We also talked about addiction and how it is a trap the enemy sets, to get us away from the plans God has for us.

This lesson is about the internet, and how it can influence and affect our lives. Cyberspace or the internet, is an entire virtual world that can have a huge impact on our thought life. While there are great things we can access online, it can also lead to bad habits and addictions.

CYBERSPACE

As most of you know, cyberspace, is the realm of computer communication. Basically, it's a virtual world that you access when you get on your iPad, your smartphone, your computer, Kindle or devices like that. A lot of your Xboxes and game systems can get on the internet as well.

Simply spending too much time on any of these devices can be harmful to your mind. Things we do on our devices can cause our brains to be stimulated, or amped up, or energized. But this is a different type of brain stimulation than when you are reading or doing math or trying to solve problems. Obviously, right? It's certainly much more fun to play a game or watch YouTube than to do your homework. One reason for that may be that it causes your brain to release excessive amounts of dopamine. If you remember from our last lesson, dopamine is the reward or pleasurable feeling that is released in our brains, that sends a signal to tell us to do something again. Dopamine is a good thing, but if we aren't careful, we can fall into addictive patterns online, because of the way our brain works.

If solving a math problem releases 1 shot of dopamine as a reward for your accomplishment, and playing a game on your phone or iPad also releases 1 shot of dopamine, but every other second, naturally you would much rather play that game. The problem is, the more you train your brain in cyberspace, especially your growing brain, and the more you are focused on the constant stimulation, the harder it may be to create pathways of natural thought, problem solving and social skills, because your brain is craving that cyber stimulation. It is so much easier to pick up your device and be stimulated, than to pick up your homework, but obviously you need to do your homework.

There is a generation of youth who got smartphones fairly young, before parents realized how harmful they could be. Years of too much screen time, or whatever they were playing, reading or looking at online, was much easier than communicating with friends and others. Many of them lack the ability or even desire to engage with people. Often you will see a group of kids together but all looking at their phones. If you don't develop the pathways in your brain to socialize with others during your teenage years, it can affect relationships you were intended to have.

Another example may be playing sports or gymnastics. When you score a basket or when you do a cartwheel you get a sense of pleasure or reward for your accomplishment. **God gave us this reward system to keep us moving forward in life and to motivate us to be the best we can.** If you feel that same sense of accomplishment just from tapping some buttons on a screen, you may find you aren't motivated to do much else.

I like video games. I enjoy playing Nintendo, my kids have iPads, and I have an iPhone. I also have to set limits with myself from scrolling on my phone because sometimes it's just so easy to be entertained by it, as opposed to doing anything else. For me, scrolling on my phone or on the internet can seem like a great escape when I don't want to deal with things around me. The problem is, this isn't the best way to spend my time, and my responsibilities don't just disappear.

Protecting your mind, by monitoring how much time you spend on your device, is important. **Experts say, as little as one hour per day of screen time can rewire or change the way your brain works.** An hour online passes faster than you think!

Just like in the world around us, there are very bad things online. While you are growing up, your parents do their best to protect you from a lot of the bad things in the world. But once you start getting online, even if they have tried to protect you with apps, filters and safeguards, things can still harm you.

ONLINE PREDATORS AND VIDEO GAME VIOLENCE

One danger is, while communicating with someone online

they may pretend to be someone they aren't. Someone can act like a kid or your friend and it may not be them. You can never, ever, ever meet up with someone that you have met online. It is hard to imagine, but there are people called predators out there. An online predator is often an adult with bad intentions toward a teenager or child. They know how to say all of the right things to try and get you to trust them, and you cannot ever think it's ok, because it isn't. To protect yourself from this, you should always tell an adult if someone tries to talk to you in a suspicious way. And never give out any information about where you live to anyone online ever, even if you think it's a trusted friend. You should not play games, text, chat or communicate online with anyone that you don't know for certain who they are, and it can be hard to know for sure who you are communicating with.

Some games have violence in them. The more you play those games the more normal violence can seem to you. Of course you know just because you can shoot someone on a game obviously doesn't mean you can in reality. However, if you excessively play violent games, your brain can be rewired, and it may become harder to separate the two realities and you may find yourself being frustrated more easily and more prone to anger and violence. Many of these games are made with the intention of creating an addiction to them. While they can be super fun, it is important that you keep a check on the time you are spending playing them.

PORNOGRAPHY

The greatest threat of the internet is **PORNOGRAPHY.**

If you don't know already, pornography is **pictures, cartoons or videos of peoples private parts used in a way that is designed to stimulate or excite your mind or brain and to bring up feelings in your body.** These images completely distort the way God intended us to view our bodies and what we do with them. These pictures are wrong, and they are dangerous.

God created our bodies and He made them beautiful in His image. The private parts of your body are just that, they are *private*. It is normal to be curious about your private parts or to be curious about others private parts. God designed you with healthy desires and feelings in your body about sex. As you mature, those desires will grow and you can learn how to manage those feelings. However, the enemy wants to take what you are curious about and use it to degrade, or pervert, the plans, purposes and desires God put inside you. One way he wants to do this is to get you hooked on pornography.

Images that are pornographic, are pictures, cartoons or videos of people naked or of people performing sexual acts. These pictures can be found in magazines or books but most often are viewed online. Images of people exposing themselves in these ways, demeans and takes away the value God has placed on us and our bodies. You are not designed to be looked at in this way nor are you made to look at others in the way that pornography compels you to. God made your body to be sacred and special.

The only thing worse than pornography is child pornography. Child pornography is when adults abuse children and take or view pictures or videos of them in a sexual manner. Child pornography is illegal and is a crime that can be given the harshest punishments under the law because it is so wrong, vile and dangerous.

One reason all pornography is dangerous, is because it is **EXTREMELY ADDICTIVE.** Just like with drugs, pornography can release excessive amounts of dopamine which can easily trick you into a habit. Looking at pornography stimulates your mind and can also stir up feelings in your body.

My friend's 7-year-old little girl accidentally clicked on something that was pornographic and she was too young to understand what it was. She didn't like the pictures and she didn't understand them, but they brought up all kinds of feelings and curiosity in her, so she kept looking at them. She started hiding her habit from her parents. She found herself thinking about the images she had seen constantly, then she would feel really bad and yucky inside. She started becoming depressed and sad. She started acting out because she felt out of control. She was so relieved when she got caught because she needed help to stop this habit that she hated. This is why God says we must protect what we see, for it affects our heart!

Viewing pornography is giving the enemy an open door into your heart. Pornography itself is a lie and it takes the sacred act of love in sex, and turns it into something profane. The enemy takes what God made to be beautiful and violates it with pornography. Pornography perverts or twists something God made to be pure and good, into something dark and unclean.

YOU ARE NEVER MEANT TO SEE SOMEONE ELSE HAVING SEX

The enemy will lie to you to get you to look at pornography. He will tell you that you need to see it so that you can learn about it, or that just a little bit won't hurt anything and that no one will ever know. The problem is, once you have seen it, your thoughts have been intruded in a way you can't take back.

The way pornography portrays sex is wrong. People who view porn often have an unrealistic idea of what sex is like. Not only is it unrealistic, but it turns people with real feelings and emotions and makes them into objects or things to be used in bad ways. Often pornography involves abusive behavior or people hurting others.

While pornography can stimulate your mind and body in a way that initially "feels good", feelings of guilt, shame and condemnation almost always follow. **While God will convict your heart to stop looking at pornography, He will never**

shame you. Shame is a feeling of regret and guilt that eats away at your heart. Shame makes you feel that you ARE your sin and that you are bad. Shame is a feeling the enemy wants you to live with. Once you start down the road of shame, you may easily begin to hate yourself. That is the very opposite of what God wants for you.

Sadly, chances are, someone may show you pornography, or you may accidentally see it. You can type the wrong word, click the wrong button and be exposed to pornography. Whatever it is, you immediately need to shut it down, turn away, and if you can, let someone know. It's important that you make a choice to protect yourself even if you are curious, and to not go back. That one choice can save you from a lot of struggling and heartache.

Many people started viewing pornography before the age of 10. Some may be older but either way, if it isn't dealt with it may cause problems in their life. Some people addicted to porn end up getting divorced, or even worse, committing sexual crimes against others. Pornography is a serious epidemic in our culture today.

The enemy wants to hijack your destiny, or the plans and purposes God has for you, by hooking you into the trap of pornography. If you have already seen pornography, whether by accident or on purpose, I am so sorry you have been exposed to it. The internet is full of tricks and clicks to get you to see it, often even when you are being careful.

God gives us a new day, every day, to start over, to be redeemed and restored. Because of Jesus, you are not only forgiven, but washed clean of all guilt and shame when you repent, or turn away from what you now know is wrong.

As we said, we lay pathways in our minds. Unfortunately, pornographic images can be really hard to stop thinking about. BUT GOD, can give you a renewed mind and will help you get those thoughts out of your head if you ask Him. And keep asking Him.

THE VERY THINGS THE ENEMY WANTS US TO HIDE ARE THE THINGS WE NEED TO SPEAK OUT

If you have been looking at pornography, you should let someone know. I pray that God will give you the courage to talk to someone that won't make you feel ashamed, but will give you the help and guidance you need. No matter how strong you think you can be, you need someone to help you. No amount of looking at porn is ok or good for you. Letting someone know what you are dealing with may be the first step to your freedom.

No matter what the case, bring God into your life on the internet. Invite Him to speak to your heart by the Holy Spirit, your inside BFF, and to lead you into safe places and to protect you.

I love that God made our minds so that they can be renewed and restored. I love that He gives us all of the tools we need to overcome anything that the enemy tries to use to harm us. When you receive Jesus, your mind belongs to Him. While we may have struggles in our thought life, when we remember who we belong to, and we take our thoughts captive and submit them to Him, those dark thoughts have to go.

The enemy wants us to conform or be like what the world says is good. The world is advertising pornography like it's no big deal, when it is a violation of God's design for us. The enemy is the author of pornography and he wants to get you hooked.

God wants us to be transformed or changed as we grow and become more and more like Him. As we do this, our lives become full of meaning and purpose. We will talk more about the feelings and desires you have or will have about sex. God has a plan for your life, and it's a great one, but He gives you choices, to choose His way or the world's way.

Protecting ourselves starts with protecting our mind-gate. Let's be intentional about what we allow in and about how much time we are spending online. There are many great things we can do online. If you have parents that limit and monitor your online use, you should know it's because they want to protect you. You can set a standard for what you are going to use the internet for and stick to it. You can make sure that if you stumble onto something you know isn't good for you, you immediately get out of that, and don't go back. You can always talk to God about what you are thinking about or struggling with, and ask for His help. He loves to help you because He loves you so much.

Romans 6:12-13

Sin is a dethroned monarch; so you must no longer give it an opportunity to rule over your life, controlling how you live and compelling you to obey its desires and cravings.

So then, refuse to answer its call to surrender your body as a tool for wickedness. Instead, passionately answer God's call to keep yielding your body to Him as one who has now experienced resurrection life! You live now for His pleasure, ready to be used for His noble purpose.

Luke 11:34

Your eye is the lamp of your body. When your eyes are healthy, your whole body is full of light.

DISCUSSION
FAMILY OR GROUP

- Do you feel you are spending too much time looking at a screen?
- What are some things you spend time doing online that may be wasteful?
- What are some good things you can use the internet for?
- Has anyone ever tried to talk to you or your friends online in a way that you felt was inappropriate?
- Has something ever popped up or you stumbled on

something you wish you hadn't seen, or you felt was wrong?

- Have you seen images that you want to get out of your mind, or are you struggling with the habit of pornography?
- Take some time to write down what you believe God thinks about pornography.
- Take some time to write what you think about pornography.
- Pray or write down anything you want God to help you with online.

PRAYER
FOR KIDS OR TEENS WHO HAVE BEEN LOOKING AT PORNOGRAPHY

Father, thank You for Your love and grace and thank You for exposing the darkness and lie of pornography. Thank you Jesus, that you died to set me free of the snare of pornography. Thank you that nothing separates me from your love and it is your desire to cleanse my mind and heart of things that bring confusion, perversion and pain to my life. Forgive me Father for anything I have seen that violates your plans and purposes for me. Help me to turn away and never go back to looking at things I shouldn't. Wash my mind with your light and love. Help me to keep my mind fixed on You.

Psalm 51
Erase my guilt by your saving grace
Create a new, clean heart within me.
Fill me with pure thoughts and holy desires, ready to please you.
Thank You for giving me a new day and for a fresh start.
Thank You for forgiving me! In Jesus precious name, Amen.

PRAYER
FOR PROTECTION FOR ALL KIDS, TEENS AND ADULTS

Father thank You that Your plans for our lives are better than we can imagine. Thank You that You have given us the power and strength to follow You and Your ways. Thank You that we can trust You to know what is best for us. We ask for protection over our hearts and minds from pornography. Help us to understand how dangerous it is and to never go back or fall into the trap that it is. Thank You that you created us in Your image and that You died so we could be pure, holy and righteous in Your sight. In Jesus name, Amen.

Consider a *family fast* from phones and internet. Just a thought.

6

WHAT MESSAGE ARE YOU SENDING?

ONLINE COMMUNICATION, DANGERS AND SAFETY

PARENTS AND LEADERS,

If your kids do not already have social media, they will be facing the pressure to get it. It is difficult as a parent to know what to allow them access to and when. There are numerous social media apps and there is a lot of information online about them. It doesn't take long to get educated on each individual app before you allow them to have it.

I have been studying about current popular apps and have been alarmed, disturbed and astounded at what kids are doing online. Unfortunately many of these platforms are created to target youth and are set up for sneaking around parental controls. Kids today are tech savvy and know how to start secret accounts and do all sorts of things we don't know about. The attraction to many of these apps is that they can be used to send content that disappears so no parents can see it. Kids are using them to send inappropriate messages, pictures and videos. Some are set up for chatting with strangers or anonymous profiles and other dangerous activity.

While each family is unique, and will make their own personal decision about when to allow access to social media and what platforms, we need to educate, and equip them as best as we can. However, from all I have learned, the most trouble happens in middle school. Most kids at that age are simply not mature enough to handle what social media entails.

Even with safety filters and monitoring apps in place, so often kids find ways around them or find themselves in a bad situation. While there is stress involved in not being a part of social media, I have heard many parents say how stress free their child was when they removed social media from their lives.

This lesson will start a general discussion of social media, sexting and cyberbullying. We will learn the dangers of the messages we are posting or sending. I recommend printing a list of current popular social media apps with their descriptions and dangers to use for discussion.

What Message Are You Sending?
Online Communication, Dangers and Safety

We have learned about protecting our minds because what we allow in our minds can affect our lives, most importantly our heart. God's desire is that we don't conform to be like this world but that we renew our minds and be transformed to be like Him. We discussed the dangers of too much screen time and the big threat of pornography. This lesson will dig deeper into other issues we face online. We are in a battle and the enemy is out to hook us, trap us, or to trip us up and to bring trouble into our lives. But we can learn what those traps are, and learn how to avoid and overcome them.

COMMUNICATING ONLINE

We didn't have cell phones when I was growing up. I did have something called a swatch phone. It had two receivers where someone could listen in on a conversation. If we didn't tell the other person someone was listening in, it was unfair to the person on the other end. As far as I can remember, nothing too bad came from it, but it wasn't fair and it wasn't right. What and how you communicate to others can be hurtful and even dangerous. Often what is meant as a prank, or kids being mean to other kids, can cause all sorts of problems and even result in serious harm.

An old friend recently sent me a picture of a note she found that I wrote in eighth grade. I didn't remember it at all. I couldn't believe the stuff I wrote in that note. I can't imagine if more stuff I said to my friends had been recorded! So much communication happens today through texting, chatting and other apps. This gives room for some of the dumb stuff we say or do online to hurt us, come back to haunt us, or to hurt someone else.

This may surprise you, but even your parents and most adults will admit, when they were growing up they said and did stupid things. Again, your brain is not fully developed and often kids and teens speak and act impulsively, or without thinking about or understanding the consequences of what they are saying or doing.

SOCIAL MEDIA

Social Media is websites or apps that enable users to create and share content or to participate in social networking. Your social network is basically your friend list or people you allow access to your personal information. There are many popular social media platforms or apps. If you don't have social media or you haven't faced pressure to get social media, most likely you will.

Some things kids and teens do on social media is send pictures or messages that they believe disappear. Other apps offer free texting, voice chatting, video sharing or live streaming, which is a live video in real time. These messages, chats, pictures and videos can be shared with all of your "friends" on the same network, with the public, which means anyone can see them, or privately with one other person or private groups.

There is a popular app where users can create videos to songs or make up their own music and share with friends or all other users of the app. The content in the songs is often explicit and contains profanity. Unfortunately there are tons of videos of little kids singing and dancing to sexually explicit songs. Most likely they have no idea what they are doing and how dangerous it can be. They also don't understand there are predators or people with bad intentions that may be watching their videos.

Other apps offer the set up of anonymous profiles, which is where you make up a name or you act like someone else. You may be talking to someone you think is a young girl, but it could be an older man. **All social media can be trolled by predators and pornography is on all social media outlets.** While some platforms attempt to manage or regulate pornography, some have minimal or no restrictions.

SEXTING

Sexting is sending sexually explicit photographs or messages. Explicit means graphic pictures or videos of people either naked, their private parts or of them doing something sexual. Sexting can also be messages describing sexual acts or behavior. Sexting is a lot like pornography except it often involves someone you know. There are serious consequences to sexting.

An example of sexting would be the following story.

A 12-year-old boy has a girlfriend that is 11. They are texting back and forth and he asks her to send him a "nude". That means he wants her to send him pictures of either her breasts or her vagina. Not only is this dangerous, this is illegal.

Sexting has **emotional consequences**. While the 11-year-old girl in our story has a choice to respond or not, how she responds can impact her life dramatically. Some girls will send the nude pictures in order to get a boy to like them, or to get attention. Some kids have sent nude pictures without being asked.

For this 11-year-old girl, if she sends the picture, feelings of embarrassment, shame and regret will most likely follow. If he receives the picture, he may be excited by it at first, but he may experience guilt and shame as well. There is nothing she can do to get the picture back. It is out there forever and there is a huge chance that he is going to send it to some of his friends. Then they may send it to their friends.

Then kids at school are talking about her, maybe making fun of her and even bullying her. She may lose her friends and feel isolated and hopeless. Her picture may even get posted for hundreds of people to see. This often leads to depression, someone harming themselves or thoughts of suicide.

It isn't only girls who send nude pictures, boys do it also. Sadly, it is common for kids to send nude pictures with or without being asked.

Not only are there social and emotional consequences to sexting, but there is always the possibility of **serious legal consequences.** It is a crime to send or receive a picture or video of someone naked or of them acting in a sexual manner. It is considered child pornography and kids or teens in possession of child pornography can go to jail. Child pornography is any visual depiction, picture or video, of sexually explicit conduct involving a minor. A minor is anyone under 18. That means if you have any nude picture or video on your phone or computer or laptop of someone under 18 years old, you could go to jail. If you then sent that picture to someone else, you may face even harsher punishment for distributing child pornography. If you receive a picture like this, you can be charged with receiving child pornography, even if you didn't want the photo or ask for it.

Not only may you face jail time, but even worse, you risk

having to register as a sex offender. This is a label that is damaging for the rest of your life.

Kids often believe that because some of these messages are sent in private and they disappear after a few seconds that they will be gone forever. The thing is *they won't.* All it takes is for the other person to take a quick screenshot of the picture or message and it's saved forever. At that point they can send it to everyone they know. Kids also believe because it may be their good friend, boyfriend or girlfriend that they can trust them and that it's harmless. Not true!

If you ever receive a picture like this, you should immediately delete it! You should tell your parents or an adult you trust.

You may be wondering why anyone would do something like this. Kids and teens are often acting impulsively and looking for popularity or attention. There are also new hormones and sexual desires flowing through their minds and bodies. But nothing is worth the consequences from sexting. Never is it ok to take, send or ask for pictures like this. Never is it safe.

GROOMING

Another common thing that happens is a young boy or girl meeting someone online and chatting with them. That person then grooms them, or manipulates them into sending pictures of themselves. Grooming, is when someone seems to be a person you can trust, says a lot of the right things and makes you feel comfortable. However, their agenda is dangerous and cannot be trusted. Grooming happens with strangers or even with people you know. Again, never is it ok to send pictures like we are talking about.

There are some very important things you need to know about texting, chatting, snapping, posting, or communicating with others over the internet or by phone. It is important that you understand, **there can be extremely serious consequences to what you say and do online and by text.**

You need to know, even if it seems to disappear, **any message you send may be saved forever. Just because you hit delete, or the message appears to go away, does not mean it's gone.** There are servers, data files, clouds and other ways that deleted messages can be kept. This goes for all pictures and videos sent and received as well. **Also, anyone can take a screenshot of any picture, post or message.** You should treat every message you send, as though anyone can see.

THE POSTER TEST

Consider and remember this when posting, snapping, texting or sending any message; imagine putting your message or picture on a poster board in the hall at school. What! No way! Yes, even though it doesn't seem like it, that is an example of what can happen to your message. So often kids make mistakes or bad choices in messages they send, and it gets sent to everyone they know. Friends, boyfriends or girlfriends you believe you can trust, may end up putting a private message out there. They may send it to just one other person, and that person posts it to everyone. Give it the poster test. Make sure any message you send is something you would be comfortable with anyone or everyone seeing. This includes any comment you make on a post.

CYBERBULLYING

Let's say you are struggling with something personal and you text your friend about it. Later they get mad at you and screenshot it and send it to others. Something personal that was meant for a trusted friend is now being seen by people it wasn't intended for. This type of situation happens often and can cause a lot of harm.

Something like this happened to a teenage boy in Manchester, Tennessee. A friend of his got mad at him and posted very embarrassing messages he had sent to someone else. She shared screenshots of some of his private messages from Snapchat and Instagram. People started making fun of him, and said horrible things.

He was so devastated and humiliated, he took his own life. This boy was a victim of cyberbullying.

This story hurts my heart, and unfortunately there are many stories like this one. As mean as that was for that person to post his private messages, I don't think she intended for him to die. Sadly, this isn't the only time someone has ended their life because of something that happened online.

Cyberbullying is when someone is bullied, threatened or intimidated online. It can be kids calling names, saying horrible and hurtful things, or threatening to hurt someone. It's often a person or people picking on someone because they are different in some way. People who are bullied, are twice as likely to commit suicide and more prone to cause self-harm. If you ever hear about or see someone being bullied online or offline, you should let someone know. If you are ever a victim of being bullied, you need to tell someone immediately. Often kids don't want to tell because they fear telling will make it worse. The truth is, adults always need to be involved when there is bullying. It can be as serious as life and death.

This is a big and important discussion. These things are hard topics to talk about, and I wish they weren't a part of our world, but they are. The truth is, your choices often determine your troubles. Your middle school and high school years can be difficult at times, but making wise decisions in the face of temptation will bring reward. Making wise choices can keep you on the path of life that God intends for you.

You may be wondering why anyone would ever send or ask for inappropriate messages. Maybe you are the one who has already sent things you regret. Often we don't understand why we do the things we do, but one thing is for sure, God has grace, love and forgiveness for you.

I want you to know you were made to be adored. You were made to be looked upon with love and acceptance. You were made to be pursued by love. You were created with a longing inside your heart to be seen and known. Sometimes that need is crying out on the inside and the enemy is right there ready to trick you into doing things that you believe will fill that need.

Whatever your situation is, maybe you have been bullied, or maybe you are the one doing the mean stuff. Maybe all of this is new to you and you feel overwhelmed. God wants you to know, that He has got you. He has you and all of your thoughts, feelings and questions. He has all of your good and your bad and none of it scares Him and none of it is too big for Him to handle. He loves and adores you in a way that no other person will ever be able to compete with. He sees you and He is pursuing you and He will never stop, no matter what. All you have to do is receive it.

DISCUSSION
FAMILY OR GROUP

- Share what your thoughts are about social media.
- Share what social media you use, how often and why. Talk about specific apps and what they are used for.
- Share inappropriate things you have seen while using social media.
- Share any mean or hateful comments you have seen or received privately or publicly on social media.
- Share if you know of anyone who is being bullied online or offline.

Pray and read and declare this over your child or group.

Psalm 91:1-6

When you sit enthroned under the shadow of Shaddai, you are hidden in the strength of God Most High. He's the hope that holds me and the Stronghold to shelter me, the only God for me and my great confidence. He will rescue you from every hidden trap of the enemy, and he will protect you from false accusation and any deadly curse. His massive arms are wrapped around you, protecting you. You can run under his covering of majesty and hide. His arms of faithfulness are a shield keeping you from harm. You will never worry about an attack of demonic forces at night nor have to fear a spirit of darkness coming against you. Don't fear a thing! Whether by night or by day, demonic danger will not trouble you, nor will the powers of evil launched against you.

Psalm 91:9-16

When we live our lives within the shadow of God Most High, our secret hiding place, we will always be shielded from harm. How then could evil prevail against us or disease infect us? God sends angels with special orders to protect you wherever you go, defending you from all harm. If you walk into a trap, they'll be there for you and keep you from stumbling. You'll even walk unharmed among the fiercest powers of darkness, trampling every one of them beneath your feet. For here is what the Lord has spoken to me: Because you have delighted in me as my great lover, I will greatly protect you. I will set you in a high place, safe and secure before My face. I will answer your cry for help every time you pray, and you will feel My presence even in your time of pressure and trouble. I will be your glorious hero and give you a feast. You will be satisfied with a full life and with all that I do for you. For you will enjoy the fullness of my salvation.

7

THE ROYAL LAW OF LOVE

SELF IMAGE, HORMONES AND LOVING YOU

PARENTS AND LEADERS,

Suicide is now the second leading cause of death for ages 15-24. Anxiety, depression and mental illness are more prevalent than ever before. Serious issues like eating disorders, and self-harm are on the rise. Kids are facing pressures unlike any time in history with technology and culture today. The enemy wants to get our kids chasing the unattainable perfect body or a life that doesn't exist. The enemy wants to get them off track by the trap of comparison and the lie that they aren't good enough.

Our culture is obsessed with self, and social media has fueled the enemy's plan to get our identity wrapped up in our body image. Social media can be hard for adults to navigate and it can be dangerous and even deadly for some teens.

I have seen what many kids and teens are following and posting. Not only is it normal to show more and more skin, but the photos and videos are getting riskier and more graphic. It is common for these kids to see videos of people doing drugs, getting wasted or getting hurt or even killed just by scrolling their social media. People are posting anything and everything in order to get likes and attention.

Many kids and teens today are DESENSITIZED or nonreactive to the most heinous and horrible acts. They are getting so used to these shocking pictures and videos that they fail to recognize the harm that is taking place.

There was a teenage boy missing from a small town in 2018. His parents were devastated and desperate to find him, not knowing if he was dead or alive. Eventually they got into his social media accounts when they saw they had been active. It turned out to be a young boy who had hacked his accounts and was posing as him. This hacker was corresponding with many of the young girls from the same town that the boy and his family knew. He was asking for nude pictures and numerous young girls were sending pictures thinking they were going to the missing boy. The sad part is they saw pleas on media that the parents were desperate to find their son and they never told that they heard from him, though they believed they had. Thankfully, this boy was eventually found, but not with the help of any of his peers who knew these parents were suffering. They even thought it was ok to send him nude pictures when his life may have been in danger. This true story reveals the condition of much of our young culture.

While there are all sorts of contributing factors, the root of the problem is often self-image and identity. There is a desperate need for kids to know who they are, where they fit in, and beyond that...to love themselves. With all the pressures they are facing, if they can connect with the love of their Heavenly Father, they can overcome it all.

This chapter talks about having a healthy body image. It also lightly touches on the hormonal changes that kids face as they go through puberty. Parents, this is a great time to get more specific about what to expect during puberty. All these things need to be talked about! You can do it! We will discuss loving ourselves and loving others. We also learn how social media can play a part in our self image. We have to wake our kids up to the truth, that they are known and loved by us and in heaven, or we risk losing them to the problems of this world.

The Royal Law of Love
Self Image, Hormones and Loving You

Something every human struggles with is how they feel about themselves. As you grow up, and even once you are an adult, how you feel about yourself will have a huge affect on how you live your life. There are so many things that influence our feelings about who we are. The enemy knows if he can get you down on yourself, he can influence everything you do and he will have direct access to your life.

Your self-image is what you believe about how you look, what you are able to achieve and who you are. Basically, it's what you think of yourself.

What you believe about you will affect everything you do, what you attract, and what you become.

A big part of how you feel about yourself is your **body image or how you feel about they way you look.**

The world projects an image that says we should look a certain way. For girls, maybe it's that we should be tall and skinny with long legs. For boys, maybe it's to be big and muscular. The world says you should look fashionable and trendy and have cool clothes and a certain style. It's everywhere you turn. It's online, on TV, on every billboard and in every movie. Celebrities and models with, what appears to be, perfect bodies, are always right in front of us.

The world promotes a body image that is unattainable or something you can never achieve. Yet the enemy wants to get you chasing after that *look,* that perfect body or physique. The enemy wants to get you focused on what you don't have, or what you have too much of regarding your body. He wants to rob you of your joy today by making you insecure about your body. The enemy wants you to be focused on how much you don't like things about yourself and the way you look.

Maybe it's your friends or classmates that you always compare yourself to. Maybe you feel like you are too short or small or too skinny or fat. Most people deal with this in some way, and some deal with it overwhelmingly.

I remember when I started to have a bad body image. It was the summer after 7th grade and I was checking in at camp with my beautiful friend. We had to get on the scales when we got there, and I noticed I weighed 13 pounds more than her. That day I began to believe the lie that I was fat. Before long, I started to deeply dislike the color of my skin, my curly hair, my freckles and the curves I was getting.

You have most likely already started caring more about how you look. As you grow you will become more and more self aware. It is good to care about how you look and to want to look good. What isn't good, is when you compare how you look to others or the unattainable image the world projects.

HORMONAL CHANGES

During puberty you grow more and faster than any other time in your life, except when you were an infant. Hormones are being released from your brain that bring changes. Boys are dealing with testosterone and girls are dealing with estrogen. These hormones are not only bringing new feelings and desires but they are also changing your body. These are the hormones that will eventually turn you into an adult. Kids go through puberty at different times. Some friends may still look like kids and some are growing faster than others.

During this time you will experience a lot of things you have never dealt with before. There are personal and private things happening that can make you feel awkward, uncomfortable or embarrassed. Everyone experiences this! While it may be happening to you at a different time than your best friend, don't worry, God's timing is right.

This is a time when the enemy really wants to make you feel insecure. He wants to make you think all eyes are on your flaws or imperfections. If we let him have his way it can seem like torture! God designed you to grow up, and going through puberty is part of that. While it can be difficult at times, you are not alone and you can count on God to help you with your personal challenges.

During these changes our feelings and emotions may be stronger than we are used to. Because of the new hormones flowing through your body, you may get angry easier than before, you may feel sad or down, or you may feel excited or wild and crazy! Don't let this scare you. Puberty is a natural process that happens over a period of time.

Your face may break out, girls boobs are growing or they may start their period. Boys are getting erections because they have new hormones that cause them to think about girls boobs. An erection is when a male's penis gets hard because he is sexually excited. During puberty this can happen at different and even awkward times. You may have experienced some of this, or maybe you will, but you need to know it's okay! It's normal! It's healthy! It's good! Nothing is wrong with you! You don't need to be ashamed! You will be ok!

The enemy wants you to believe something is wrong with you, but it isn't! Don't let him win! Before you start wanting to change yourself, you need to laugh out loud about the very thing he is trying to make you feel bad about. These physical changes and feelings mean that you are experiencing the very things meant for growing up. I hope you have someone you can talk to about these things in a safe, comfortable and healthy way.

LOVING YOU

Throughout our lives we need to be aware of how we think

about ourselves. **What we think about the way we look and who we are, needs to be shaped by God.** You are an expression of God. You need to know how God sees you and you need to be reminded often! God does not compare you to others or to what is trending online or on TV. He fashioned you out of His image and He loves you perfectly just as you are.

1 John 4:19 NIV
> We love because He first loved us.

You absolutely need to connect with how God feels about you, so you can truly love yourself. No one can help you love you, the way God can. Often people look to others to make them feel good about themselves in ways that are not healthy. While it is good to be loved and seen by others, ultimately the sense of worth and confidence that you need to love yourself should come from your Father God.

Not only does God want you to love you, He wants you to love others with His love.

THE ROYAL LAW OF LOVE

James 2:8
> Your calling is to fulfill the royal law of love as given to us in this scripture: "You must love and value your neighbor as you love and value yourself!"

1. You can't love your neighbor unless you love yourself
2. God describes loving others as "your calling"

Your neighbor is everyone and anyone. You were created out of love to be loved and to love in return. Never based on how you look or what you do, but based on who made you. God is love, and He created you to reflect His nature, or to be like Him.

He is so big we can't even wrap our minds around who He is. But one thing is true, is if you look around, all of the people you see are a facet of Him. Everyone reveals something about Him, just by the way they look!

We attract people based on how we feel about ourselves.

Boys and girls, the way you treat each other, or the way you allow others to treat you, is reflected in how you feel about yourself. While you are having feelings and desires that make you want to connect with others physically and emotionally, you have a responsibility to love and value your neighbor, or that boy or that girl. You have a responsibility to honor and respect others even if they don't seem to deserve it.

GIRLS

Valuing yourself is knowing that you are God's chosen daughter. When you know you are God's girl, you dress in a way that shows you know you are loved. Showing off your body in order to get noticed by others is a sign that you don't know how valuable you are in the eyes of God. This type of attention may attract trouble and send a message that tempts others to look at you in a sexual way. Your body is beautiful, and your desire to be seen is natural, but the enemy wants to twist your desires into a trap for you and for others. It takes courage to not follow the crowd and dress and act in a way that brings the wrong kind of attention. It all starts with knowing how valuable you are, and your Heavenly Father is waiting to reveal that to you personally.

BOYS

God's chosen sons show they know they are valued when they treat girls and others with honor and respect. No matter how she is acting, or what she is wearing, or how raging your desires are, she deserves to be valued. The enemy wants you to see her for her body only but she is God's girl, and how you treat her or speak about her matters. How you treat yourself matters, and when you love you, it will show in how you treat others.

When we know we are loved and we live in such a way, we empower others to do the same!

While sometimes our differences challenge us to love others, your neighbors are those who look like you and those who don't. Your neighbor is the person that dresses weird or acts strange or even looks offensive. God tells us to love them, for real.

Proverbs 16:24

Nothing is more appealing than speaking beautiful life-giving words. For they release sweetness to our souls and inner healing to our spirits.

The way you speak to yourself is so important. If you are always having thoughts of, *I don't like my legs, I hate my hair, I don't like my teeth, or I wish I was more muscular,* you will empower those negative feelings about yourself. If you speak graciously and lovingly to yourself, your soul will feel sweet!

It's time to get in the habit of loving yourself, because you were made in the image of God and you are a facet of Him. It's time to speak kind words to yourself and embrace how God created you. If He chose this hair and this body for you, then it's right, and His ways are higher than what you think would be better.

Gracious words to others can change someone's life. When you speak kind words, give compliments, tell someone they look nice or you like their hair or outfit, you are not only bringing healing to yourself, but to them as well. Scripture tells us, so it's true!

If you are having a day where you are down on yourself, start speaking life-giving sweet words to yourself and to others, and your spirits will be lifted!

SOCIAL MEDIA AND SELF IMAGE

Another thing that can influence how we think about ourselves is social media. When you are scrolling through social media you are seeing the highlights of everyone's day or life. We see how beautiful and good looking everyone is and how much fun they are having with their friends. Maybe you aren't having the best time with your friends or you aren't on a fabulous trip. Or maybe you didn't get invited to the party that looks like everyone is having a blast at. The point is, comparison is a trap! Something about social media just begs for us to compare our lives or our looks to others, and this can cause us to feel bad about ourselves.

Our culture today has become obsessed with image. Specifically the image presented on social media. This isn't just with kids and teens, this includes adults.

I know a woman who is a star on social media. She has a lot of followers. She is always posting beautiful and posed pictures of herself. She usually adds something meant to be encouraging or inspiring but the point of her post seems to be all about attention. People are commenting how wonderful, gorgeous and amazing she is. While she may get thousands of likes, and have what appears to be a glamorous lifestyle, I happen to know her real life doesn't look like that. I'm also not sure she has many real friendships. She is very beautiful and can make a great post, but it seems like her identity is found in the attention she gets for the way she looks. What will happen to her self worth when she gets old and her looks fade, or if people quit liking her posts?

You were made to connect with others and to get to know them personally. You were made to be known and seen beyond how you look or the image that you put out. The enemy is out to steal real friendships by replacing them with the counterfeit of social media friends. And he wants you to believe the lie that the amount of attention you get from a picture you post is where you find your self worth.

Every time my family goes to the beach we see teenage girls spending tons of time trying to get the right pose in their bikini in front of the ocean. They are sucking it in or sticking it out so they can get all the compliments and likes. Often when you see posts like this, the comments are full of "you are so hot", or "you are so skinny." Despite the girls being on a fun vacation, they are spending all this time to get hundreds of likes based on how their bodies look.

I have seen the other side, where girls and boys post pictures to get likes, and the hateful comments start rolling in. People are being body shamed, or made fun of online constantly. Often what was made as an innocent post, becomes an open door for others to cause hurt and humiliation. You should never be the one posting comments meant to make fun of or tear down anyone. Always go by the Golden Rule. How would you feel if someone said that about you?

Selfies are cute and fun, but the trouble is when your focus is too much on yourself. While God wants us to love ourselves and care about how others see us, there is a healthy way to do that. Your desire to look good is great! But our culture today has become obsessed with themselves and that goes for adults too.

People are doing crazy things to get *likes* or attention. Some have literally died for the attention they are seeking. According to a study published in the Journal of Family Medicine and Primary Care, between October of 2011 and November of 2017, atleast 259 died while taking a selfie. These mostly occurred by people taking dangerous risks to get a lot of likes. People were killed posing with guns and accidentally shooting themselves, people fell off of cliffs, were washed away in the waves or crashed their car while taking a selfie.

Many people mistake the amount of likes on social media, or attention they get, for their self-worth. Many people mistake their social media friends as their actual friends, when it's never meant to replace real life connections with others.

The point is, attention, online or offline, may feel good for a moment, but it only appeals to what's on the outside, it doesn't fulfill what's on the inside. It won't satisfy the very thing you are longing for.

We all desire to be seen and known by others and by God. Being seen isn't about what people see when they look at you, it's about people knowing the *real* you. We all desire to be loved and to love in return, not based on our looks or our flesh, but based on who we are in God.

Romans 8:5-6

Those who are motivated by the flesh only pursue what benefits themselves. But those who live by the impulses of the Holy Spirit are motivated to pursue spiritual realities. For the mind-set of the flesh is death, but the mind-set controlled by the Spirit finds life and peace.

When our minds are set on ourselves or our "selfies" we will pursue the wrong things. Being focused on yourself will lead you down the wrong path. Trying to achieve feeling good about yourself because of what is on the outside will leave you chasing something that will never satisfy.

True beauty comes from our Creator. He thought you up and formed you and He loves you. The only perfect body is the one you have right now at this moment. Not the one five pounds less or more defined. Don't let the enemy convince you to chase something that doesn't exist. God wants you to receive His love, love Him in return, love yourself and love others. He wants your growing up years to be filled with confidence in Him and in yourself. He wants you to see how amazing He made you so that you can achieve the very things He put in your heart to achieve. Will you do that?

DISCUSSION
PARENTS AND LEADERS

- Share struggles you had with your self image growing up and now.
- Share things you see that you love about the outside and inside of your child or group.
- Share things you feel God highlighting about them that He loves.

KIDS

- Share things you love about your parents or leaders.
- Share what you love about them on the outside and the inside.
- Share what you believe God sees when He looks at your parents or leaders.

FAMILY OR GROUP

- In your journal on the top of a piece of paper, write down the things you have struggled with or that you don't like about yourself. On the bottom half of that page, write down what God says about those things. If they aren't encouraging and loving, they aren't from Him.
- On the next page, write down if anyone has ever made fun of you or teased you about something and how that made you feel. Ask God to speak truth to your heart to replace the hurt from being teased. Forgive anyone that may have hurt you if you feel you need to. Share with the group or your family if you feel comfortable.
- Pray and ask God to highlight someone you know that

gets teased or may not like themselves. Write a prayer for them, or share with your family or group. Pray for them to know how much God loves them.

- Talk about ways you can speak life to yourself and to others by building them up. If you are in a group, turn to your neighbor and say something great about them.

PRAYER

Father, thank You that You are always with us and that You know everything about us. Thank You that You love us perfectly and help us to know it. Help us to be filled from the inside instead of looking for attention and affection in the wrong ways. Give us wisdom and protect us online and offline. Expose the traps the enemy wants us to step into before we stumble. Help us to love ourselves and others and to call out the best in them. Help us to see people the way you do and draw the right people to our path. Help us to glorify You by the way we love and live. In Jesus name, Amen.

Read the following scripture over your group or child. Plug in their name or the correct pronoun each time you see an underlined word. If you are leading a group, you can print out this scripture with their names in the correct place and give it to them.

Psalm 139
Lord you know everything there is to know about me.
You perceive every movement of my heart and soul, and you understand my every thought before it even
enters my mind.
You are so intimately aware of me, Lord.
You read my heart like an open book
and you know all the words I'm about to speak
before I even start a sentence!

You know every step I will take before
my journey even begins.
You've gone into my future to prepare the way,
and in kindness you follow behind me
to spare me from the harm of my past. (my mistakes)
With your hand of love upon my life,
you impart a blessing to me.
This is just too wonderful, deep, and incomprehensible!
Your understanding of me brings me wonder and strength.
Where could I go from your Spirit?
Where could I run and hide from your face?
If I go up to heaven, you're there!
If I go down to the realm of the dead, you're there too!
If I fly with wings into the shining dawn, you're there!
If I fly into the radiant sunset, you're there waiting!
Wherever I go, your hand will guide me;
your strength will empower me.
It's impossible to disappear from you,
or to ask the darkness to hide me,
for your presence is everywhere,
bringing light into my night.
There is no such thing as darkness with you.
The night, to you, is as bright as the day;
there is no difference between the two.
YOU FORMED MY INNERMOST BEING,
SHAPING MY DELICATE INSIDE
AND MY INTRICATE OUTSIDE,
and wove them together in my mother's womb.
I thank you, God, for making me so mysteriously complex!
Everything you do is marvelously breathtaking.
It simply amazed me to think about it!
How thoroughly you know me, Lord!
You formed every bone in my body
when you created me in the secret place,

carefully, skillfully shaping me from nothing to something.
You saw who you created me to be before I became me!
Before I'd ever seen the light of day,
the number of days you planned for me
were already recorded in your book.
EVERY SINGLE MOMENT YOU ARE THINKING OF ME!
How precious and wonderful to consider
that you CHERISH me constantly in your every thought!
O God, your desires toward me are more
than the grains of sand on every shore!
When I wake up each morning you're still with me.

Read this any time you are struggling with who you are and know that you are beautiful and unique in the sight of God. Your Father in heaven created you just as you are and He wants you to love yourself.

8

GOD'S DESIGN FOR SEX PART 1

COVENANT, MARRIAGE AND TEMPTATION

PARENTS AND LEADERS,

Parents, this is a great time to cover things you haven't talked about regarding sex and different types of sex. Kids and teens want to know and need to hear from us. The best thing you can do is push through the uncomfortable feelings and talk to them. If you don't know the answers, just say you don't know. That's ok! Just hearing it from you will open doors of communication and make it known that you are a safe place to talk.

Leaders, obviously you would need parents permission to speak on this issue due to its nature. During the lesson and discussion, offer note cards for kids to anonymously write questions they have, to be answered later or in the next session. Look over the questions and prepare before you answer them. If possible and appropriate, offer to stay for personal questions or prayer at the end.

There are a lot of things our kids need to know about sex that would be best if they learn from us. I have heard two of my favorite pastors speak on *the principle of first mention*. This can be applied to our kids and the first time they hear things about sex. Basically, the first thing they hear can become a belief they base everything on from that point forward. If possible, the first time they hear about things regarding sex and sexuality needs to be from us, and it needs to be based on what God says. I believe the earlier we discuss these things the better. As long as they have had "the talk", they are not too young to learn about these issues.

It can be difficult to talk to our kids about these things. They are so innocent and free, and we fear that changing. It can be uncomfortable and awkward and let's face it, we don't have all of the answers. The problem comes when we don't say anything. Silence brews shame and also invites the ways of the world to become the voice on the issue of sex and sexuality.

In the past, we have done it all wrong. When you start telling kids they shouldn't have sex before marriage just because the Bible says so, you may have already lost them. Until they have a real relationship with the Author, or an understanding of how God cares for them, that may not mean much. If you just say homosexuality is wrong, that isn't enough.

The topics discussed in the next two chapters are sensitive and even controversial. The culture we live in wildly promotes premarital sex, homosexuality and transgender lifestyle. The enemy is trying to silence the voice of Truth by accusing Christians of hate when they stand for the Word of God. While God's Word is clear on these issues, I believe so often the church has fallen into the enemy's hands by either condemning or outcasting homosexuals and the trans community. Many in the church have also partnered with the enemy by bending the truth altogether and embracing sin.

For about a year I have been seeking the Lord on this issue. I have read or listened to countless testimonies of men and women who have left the homosexual lifestyle and how God changed their hearts. I have sought to find what worked for them in or out of the church. I have wept and prayed and developed a love for homosexuals unlike I ever expected.

This is not a subject I take lightly, as I have people in my life I love deeply who are gay. For them to ever think I condemn them grieves my heart, because I don't. I know what God's word says, and I cannot deny it. The testimonies from people who have gotten free from the lifestyle have reaffirmed the Truth. These people are bold in the fact that you can never bend God's word. People need and want to hear the truth in love because that is what sets them free.

Some people think none of these things will ever apply to their family or child. I have been surprised at the things I have learned and how many kids and teens are struggling with their identity or same sex attraction.

All of this to say, God has a perfect design for sex and sexuality. While we may make many mistakes over our lifetime, His way is THE way. We need to shepherd the next generation in the way of the truth. Not just for their life but for the lives they influence.

This next two chapters cover an array of topics regarding sex but highlight what God's design is. My prayer is that this would open the door for our children to find us and the church to be a safe place to come regarding their sexuality and all of the things they are facing. I pray you would keep that door open and the conversation flowing so they always know they can come to you. I pray that your heart is challenged and encouraged by where you stand on this delicate issue. I pray that you would build up, believe in, and stand with the next generation that God's design for sex in their life is not only the best, but is possible!

God's Design for Sex Part 1
Covenant, Marriage and Temptation

When I was growing up, I had a distorted view of sex. My parents didn't talk to me about it at all, which is still pretty common. I got the impression that it was something to hide, or something that was wrong and went against God. I had no idea what God's design and intentions were for me regarding sex. I believed sex was something we shouldn't talk about and was shameful. Today, many people still have the wrong idea of what sex is all about.

I want to set the record straight. There is much to learn about God's design for sex and sexuality. One very important thing to know is **sex is a gift from God to us.** God created sex, so having sex within His design is a good thing, a healthy thing and something to be excited about.

We know that one of God's purposes for sex, was His brilliant design to populate the earth, but it is more than that! **You were created out of love, to be loved and to receive love.** You were created to feel loved and to love in return. **Sex is an expression of love designed by God to bring physical pleasure to people inside the covenant relationship of marriage.**

COVENANT

God is in the business of dealing in covenant. **Covenant means a binding agreement or a PROMISE between two people or between God and us.** God has never broken a covenant or a promise, and it is his desire that we wouldn't either.

You may know, we have the Old Testament and the New Testament of the Bible. The word testament also means covenant. In the Old Testament, God made covenant promises to His people at different times. One example of God's covenant was the rainbow He put in the sky after He flooded the whole earth, it was His promise He would never do that again.

God also used blood from sacrificed animals to seal His covenant or to show that He would be faithful to His promise. God also used blood in covenant for the forgiveness of sins. In the New Testament we have Jesus. Jesus is the perfect display of covenant. Not only does the blood He shed on the cross signify forgiveness and promise, it signifies life. You may wonder what does this have to do with sex? Everything! I learned this from my favorite preacher, Kris Vallotton, and I was blown away!

When a man and woman get married they are entering a covenant relationship with one another. The most sacred form of covenant between people on earth is the **marriage covenant**. It is quite possible that God created something to seal that covenant or promise, more than just a legal marriage agreement or a wedding ceremony.

Girls have something called a **hymen.** Girls you probably don't even know that you have it, because there doesn't seem to be any biological purpose for the hymen. **The hymen is a thin membrane about a half-inch inside the vagina that covers the external vaginal opening.**

For most girls that are **virgins, or girls that have never had sex before,** their hymen is intact or it's just there. When males or females have sex for the first time, it's referred to as losing your virginity. Typically the first time you have sexual intercourse, females will experience a small amount of vaginal bleeding due to the stretching or "breaking" of her hymen.

Could it be that God intended this blood to be like a seal of the covenant promise in marriage? I believe it is! Could it be that this blood also signifies life that will be created between these two people in the form of a family? I believe this too! It is amazing how all of creation points to God if you just look.

Once you have had sex, you cannot get your hymen or your virginity back. **God's design is for you to have sex with one person within the marriage covenant.**

Sex is so much more than an act or just physical feelings between two people. During sex, a number of hormones can be released in your body. One of those hormones is **oxytocin.** Oxytocin is known as the bonding hormone. This hormone is also released when a mom breast feeds her baby or when you snuggle or cuddle with someone. Oxytocin has been called the "love hormone". The purpose of this is for a sense of unbreakable connection. When two souls come together and are united as one in the act of sex, they are forming a bond on a deep emotional level. This is a bond that is not meant to be broken.

In Genesis 2:24, it describes Adam and Eve as two becoming one flesh. Which is exactly what happens when two people come together as one when they have sex. Right after that it says, they felt no shame. Why did God see it necessary to put that there?

Shame is a painful emotion caused by the awareness of guilt or a feeling of humiliation, embarrassment or deep regret.

It is never God's desire for you to be shamed! Quite the opposite. However, shame is a real emotion that you may feel when you have any kind of sex outside of His design. Until Adam and Eve were outside of God's will, they felt no shame.

When Adam and Eve ate from the wrong tree in the garden, they knew they had done wrong and they hid from God. For the first time they wanted to cover themselves, because they were embarrassed or ashamed of themselves.

The enemy loves to use shame in people's lives. He loves to get you to take on shame and to hide from God or to run from God because of things you feel you have done wrong or sin in your life. He will also try to shame you when you have done nothing wrong. Either way shame is a lie!

If you have any sexual sin in your life, or if you are having normal sexual desires and the enemy is using it to shame you, instead of running from God, it is time to run to God! Your sin does not scare Him away. God is never ever, ever, ever, ever ashamed of you no matter what you have done! The enemy wants you to think that you have messed everything up for good but God wants you to know that His grace and mercy is new every day, and He can make all things new if you follow Him.

God's ways are higher than ours. He knows everything. Because He loves us so much He gives us a plan for sex that is pure and beautiful and good. His perfect plan does not involve hurt or guilt or shame. **When we follow His design for sex in** our lives we are protecting ourselves from allowing the enemy or others to hurt us in so many ways.

SEXUAL ABUSE

If anyone has ever touched you or abused you in any way sexually, they have violated you in the worst way that no one should ever have to experience. Even if it is someone you love and care about, what they are doing or have done is wrong and dangerous. Sexual abusers prey on children or teens and use them in a way that is for their own sexual pleasure. Abusers often threaten kids and fear keeps them from telling the truth, but someone needs to know about it immediately. If this is happening or has ever happened to you, it is not your fault and you must tell someone! Or if you know of someone who is being abused, you must get help right away!

Sex is meant to be a beautiful gift from God that is to be adored, cherished, protected, valued, honored, treasured, sacred and safe. This very much describes the way God loves you. He adores you, cherishes you, treasures you, values you, honors you and wants to protect you and keep you safe. However, in the world we live in things don't always go the way God would choose. God never wants sex to be belittled, devalued, cheapened, perverted or abused. Unfortunately, we live in a world where all of those things are happening. If we aren't listening to what God is saying to us about sex, we will fall into what the world says.

The world wants to pervert Gods plan for sex in exchange for the enemies plan. The world wants you to believe that sex is about you, your pleasure and nothing else. The world wants you to think you need to experience all kinds of sex with all kinds of people. The world wants to devalue sex by saying it doesn't mean anything and by telling you the lie that you aren't bonded with someone when you have sex with them. The world wants to

REMOVE love from sex. The world wants to remove covenant or marriage from sex.

All of these lies are being displayed on TV, in movies, and all over the internet. They are glamorizing sex outside of marriage in a way that makes it appealing and sends a message that anything is acceptable. Having sex outside of God's design opens you up to struggles that can affect your heart, your mind and your soul.

You were created as a sexual being to be loved in a physical way. You were created to be touched, hugged, kissed and loved on intimately. God designed your body in a way that you will have a desire for sexual pleasure. It is healthy and beautiful to have those desires, but you must learn how to manage them and you can do that with His help and His strength.

People often refer to your sexual urges and desires as your **sex drive.** As you go through puberty and mature, your sex drive may increase and this is normal, and healthy. God designed you to want to have sex! If you are experiencing those desires, do not be ashamed!

You have to be intentional about how you manage those feelings and desires instead of letting them drive you!

TEMPTATION

You are going to be faced with temptations to have sex before you get married. Those temptations can be difficult when you enter into relationships as boyfriend and girlfriend. Your feelings can be great, or they can be terrible, but one thing they shouldn't be, is the driving force that tells you what to do. We can't live by the philosophy: *do whatever you feel,* or very quickly we will be on a path of destruction!

You are the one in charge of your body and can set boundaries to protect yourself. You do not have to allow someone to touch you sexually or have sex with you. People may do and say all kinds of things to convince you that you should, but no one has the right to make that decision but you. Again, if anyone has ever violated you in a sexual way, someone needs to know.

I want to encourage you to ask God to help you decide the boundaries for your life and your body within relationships. You may not have a boyfriend or girlfriend now, but someday you will and it is key that YOU set boundaries in place to make it easier for you to follow God's plan. You may have already crossed boundaries or allowed someone else to, it is NEVER TOO LATE to start over, and have boundaries from this day forward.

This is something you can pray about, ask God for His direction and clarity, and keep this in your heart as you grow up.

A good example may be, if you have a boyfriend or girlfriend, you choose not to be alone together. Being alone opens the door to kissing and touching and the temptation can become so strong, your feelings take over and convince you that you don't have to do the right thing. Setting a boundary is making a decision about where you stand, before you find yourself in the middle of making a difficult choice.

Song of Songs 8:4 NIV
> Daughters of Jerusalem, I charge you: Do not arouse or awaken love until it so desires.

Girls, it takes courage and bravery not to follow the crowd in the way you present yourself. If you are flirting and teasing and tempting boys, even by the clothes you are wearing, you may be opening yourself up to a specific type of attention and it will make setting boundaries much more difficult. It also takes courage to say no to sex despite that fact that the boy you like really wants you to do it.

Boys, just because she is dressed a certain way or acting flirtatious, does not mean you can throw respect and honor for her out the window. The world wants you to look at people as objects of your desire and that is a lie. Remember, that is God's girl, no matter how she is acting. Being brave means not going along with the crowd and trying to get a girl just because you can or just because that's what others are doing.

When you let your feelings lead your actions, you are setting yourself up for trouble. The enemy will tell you, "He or she won't like me if I don't have sex with them or let them do what they want with me." If someone is asking, urging, pushing or trying to get you to do sexual things with them, while it feels great to be pursued or wanted, and while it may be tempting, it doesn't feel great to be used for physical pleasure.

The enemy will also try to convince you because everyone else is doing it, it's normal and part of life and it's not a big deal. Sex is the biggest deal. What you do with your body is so important to your life. You are a big deal to God, and He values you and your body and wants you to value and love yourself and others. He wants you to have respect for yourself and He wants you to be with someone that also respects you, and cherishes you.

SEX OUTSIDE OF MARRIAGE

The enemy will tell you there is no way you can wait until marriage to have sex. Let me say that again, the enemy WILL tell you there is no way you can wait until marriage to have sex. The world will tell you that, even your friends or adults may tell you that. That is a lie! Believing one lie, opens the door for the next one to come in. So often, once people have lost their virginity outside of marriage, they decide it doesn't matter who they have sex with. Another lie! Just because you have crossed boundaries before or have already lost your virginity, does not mean it doesn't matter if you have sex with other people. You can always start over and protect yourself going forward.

It may not be easy, but choosing to protect your virginity, will bring God's blessing on you and ultimately your marriage in a way that is beyond your expectations. As you protect and value yourself and your future marriage, you will be rewarded!

God designed you to be loved and pursued, but that is about so much more than just physical pleasure.

Your Heavenly Father loves you so much He wants to protect you from hurt and pain. When two people come together as one outside of marriage, they are tying their souls together emotionally in a way that can bring a lot of grief. This isn't just for girls. Boys feel this emotional bond as well. When you haven't committed your life to the other person in marriage, there will be heartache. Some people may deny and bury their pain, but those wounds are there. Your heart is involved in the act of sex whether you want it to be or not. If you break up, your heart can literally feel broken or like a death is occurring. When the other person starts dating someone else, you may feel betrayal and hurt unlike you can imagine. God didn't wire us to share the intimate, vulnerable and the deeply personal experience of sex, outside of marriage.

You may really like, or even be in love with, your boyfriend or girlfriend. You may think someday you will marry them, but that isn't the same as the covenant that is actually made in marriage.

SEXUALLY TRANSMITTED DISEASES

There are other risks involved in sex. **Sexually Transmitted Diseases** are infections that are passed from one person to another through sexual contact. There are over 20 different kinds of STDs. Some can be treated, and some cannot, and you live with them forever. Anyone can get an STD. Some are spread from skin to skin and you don't even have to have sex to contract them.

CONDOMS

Often during sex men wear a condom to protect them from

getting an STD or from getting someone pregnant. A **condom is a thin rubber sheath worn over the penis during sexual intercourse to prevent conception (or pregnancy) or sexually transmitted diseases.**

While condoms can reduce your risk for some of these diseases and can protect from getting pregnant if used correctly, there are still risks that come with condom use. They don't always get used properly, or they malfunction, and then they aren't protecting against anything. There are diseases that condoms do not protect against even when worn properly, despite what many people think or say.

PREGNANCY

Another obvious issue with having sex outside of marriage is the possibility of pregnancy. Teenagers and young unmarried adults get pregnant all the time. Any child's life is a gift from God. Any child born to a married or unmarried mother, is a life to value and cherish and love. The challenges of having a baby are beyond what you can understand until you actually have one. God's desire for all of His children is that they would be in a family with a mom and a dad. Family was God's idea.

Many of you, including myself, come from a broken home, or a divorced family. Some of you may have never met your mother, or father. Some of you may be adopted. You may live with your grandparents or maybe you have lost a parent. You may have two moms or dads. There is not a perfect family. ALL families are loved by God, no matter what they look like! However, the struggles and the pain that come from broken homes or from parents that make big mistakes is indisputable.

Girls, if you ever get pregnant before you get married, God is big enough to walk you through it. While that may not be the path you would choose for your life, GOD WILL meet you where you are, He will provide for you and sustain you. **Abortion, or** having a medical procedure to terminate or end a pregnancy, is the most painful choice of all. God is the author of life, and ending the life of a baby in the womb is never a good choice. Many girls and women have suffered the deepest pain and regret from making the choice of abortion. The world will tell you it's ok to have an abortion, but your heart will tell you the truth, abortion ends a life. Some of the bravest young girls that have gotten pregnant before they were ready to be moms have given their babies up for adoption. This is a difficult yet courageous choice.

There are long term affects to having pre-marital sex. God did not design you to have sex with multiple people. The enemy wants you to open yourself up to relational confusion, chaos, guilt and shame by treating sex casually. Some day when you do get married, your husband or wife will want to know that you are totally committed to them in a way you have never been with anyone else. One way is by saving yourself in that intimate and special way for them only. By waiting to have sex, you are protecting the future of your family. By waiting to have sex, you are eliminating many areas that the enemy uses against marriage.

All of this talk about sex is NOT meant to overwhelm you. While this is a lot of heavy stuff, when we follow God's design, we don't have to deal with most of these things. That is why God's way is the best! He loves us and He wants to keep us protected, safe and feeling loved in the purest way.

Sex inside the covenant of marriage is fun, feels good, and is the most intimate thing that happens between a husband and wife. God wants you to look forward to having sex because He created you that way. He wants you to know that He has given you everything you need to manage your desires as you walk with Him. He also wants you to know that if you make mistakes, or do things you regret, He is standing there with open arms, ready to forgive you, to cleanse you, and to walk with you as you set boundaries and make wise choices for your life. God's design for

sex is a beautiful act that He looks upon with delight and blessing. When you follow His design you will be blessed!

DISCUSSION
PARENTS AND LEADERS

- Open up for any questions or thoughts to be shared.
  Talk over the main points of the lesson.
- Share how you had wrong ideas about sex when you
  were growing up.
- Share if your parents talked to you about sex and what
  they said.
- Share your heart personally for your child or group
  regarding God's design for sex.

KIDS

- If you have anything bothering you about sex, write it
  down or share with the right person.
- If you have any sexual sin that you want forgiveness
  for, simply pray and ask God for that.
- Take some quiet time and write down what you think
  about sex and what you feel God is saying to you
  about it.
- Write out a prayer you have to God about sex, it's
  between you and Him.

PRAYER

*Thank you Father, for giving us the gift of sex. Thank you for
designing us to be pure and blameless through Jesus. Help us to see sex
the way you do and to bring honor to you by the way we live our lives.*

Father, help us to see the lies of the enemy regarding sex that bring hurt and pain into our lives. Expose the traps the enemy sets that will get us going down a dark path sexually. Father help us to know the truth and to be set free by it! Father bring friends and support alongside of us that can build us up and encourage us on the journey for purity.

9

GOD'S DESIGN FOR SEX PART 2

HOMOSEXUALITY, GENDER CONFUSION AND FREEDOM

HOMOSEXUALITY

ONE OF THE most difficult issues to discuss is **homosexuality, or being attracted to, or sexually desiring someone of the same sex.** This is a very delicate subject and has been a painful journey for so many who have been outcast by their families or mistreated by the church or Christians. Same sex attraction, or being attracted to someone who is of the same sex as you, is a real struggle and one that needs to be dealt with in the most loving way!

Many of you know this, but a homosexual man may be referred to as gay, and a homosexual woman may be called a lesbian. The word gay can be used in general to describe someone who is homosexual. Someone who refers to themselves as **bisexual, is a person sexually attracted to both men and women.**

There are many passionate opinions in this world about the issue of homosexuality. It is an issue that is personal to me, as several people I love dearly are gay. There isn't one thing they could ever do that would stand in the way of my love for them.

More importantly, God feels that way, *times a million*. These people are awesome and amazing. They have adopted children, who I also love so much, and they have given them more of a life than many traditional families have.

All of that being said, God is very clear on His plan and design for sex and marriage. There are places in scripture where God specifically addresses homosexuality. He calls it immoral and clearly refers to it as sin. It comes down to either believing what God's Word says, or not believing it. God created marriage to be between a man and woman, Genesis 2:24. God's Word is clear in the Old and New Testament.

Anything outside of God's design, whatever it looks like, is a sin. God knew that this would be an area where the enemy or the world would distort His truth. God warns us to not be deceived.

Some churches today are embracing the homosexual lifestyle and this goes against the Word of God that never changes and remains forever.

There is a common phrase in the world today. Love is love. The implication is that you can be with whoever you desire, man or woman, girl or boy, in or out of marriage doesn't matter. But the truth is, God is love, and loving God means obeying His commands and He defines what is acceptable and pleasing. The enemy is trying to pervert what God's design is for sex, marriage, and relationships.

This is not to say that homosexuals don't love each other. Many people living the gay lifestyle are kind loving people. If you are a Christian and you are condemning people based on their sexual preference, you are doing just what the enemy wants! I believe it is God's desire for Christians and churches to be a people and a place where anyone, gay or straight, can encounter God's love and presence. It is not our job to change people, it is our job to love them and invite them into a relationship with God who is the one who transforms hearts. Loving them also means not bending the truth, even when that's hard. That means, not being afraid to say that we believe what God says about homosexuality. When we love the way God loves us, hearts change, people change.

If you are struggling with same sex attraction, you are not alone. Same sex attraction does not mean you are homosexual. If you have experimented sexually with someone of the same sex, that does not make you gay. If you are a boy that is more feminine or a girl that is like a tomboy, that also does not mean you are gay. These are things that the enemy can use to hook you into believing a lie.

If you believe you are gay, you are fully loved by God, and nothing will change that. His ways are higher than ours, and He will never abandon you. He is your Father and your creator and you are defined by Him and not by your desires or preferences.

I pray for God to give you the courage to share what you are feeling. The enemy wants us to hide in fear. Shame keeps us in the dark. No matter what you are going through, you aren't meant to go through it alone.

My hope is that the church will be a safe place for anyone struggling with same sex attraction. Not by bending the truth for our desires, but by coming alongside of us, loving us, and letting God reveal Himself personally to us in this area.

You may not have heard of this much, because the world wants to hide it, but many former homosexuals are being changed by the love of Jesus and coming out as straight. There are resources where you can find answers, acceptance and encouragement that lead you to freedom.

The world will tell you no one can define you but you. Your feelings, desires, wants or attractions, should never define you! If we are lead by whatever we want or feel, whenever, however, we are opening ourselves up to a life of sin, darkness and death! Not just with our sexuality but with anything.

Another area where the world is changing the narrative of what God created, is with **gender.** Your sex is either male (a boy), or female (a girl). Most of you know this and would be surprised at the thought of it being any different. However, there is a growing trend in this world that is saying *you aren't who God made you to be.* The belief is that you can be whoever, or whatever... whenever, and that you can change your gender or your sex.

TRANSGENDERISM

A transgender person is someone who identifies as someone of the opposite sex. An example is, a person is born a girl, but thinks she should be a boy. She feels like she is a boy, and therefore she starts to dress like one, act like one and maybe even change her name.

A transsexual, is a person that permanently transitions into the gender with which they identify, usually with medical assistance. So the girl that was born a girl, but "identifies" as a boy, starts to take medicine or hormones that make her take on boy features. She may grow hair in new places, start shaving, get bigger muscles, and look much more like a male. Then she may have surgery to have her breasts removed.

A person who is **gender fluid,** is someone who prefers to remain flexible about their gender, rather than committing to a single one. This person may sometimes be a boy, and sometimes a girl, based on however they feel.

YOUR GENDER IS WHAT GOD GAVE YOU, NOTHING CAN CHANGE THAT.

Naturally, boys and girls may wonder what it is like to be the opposite sex, but this doesn't mean they are transgender. There are people who consistently struggle with feeling like they aren't the sex they were born with or who God created them to be. These people are often referred to as having a condition called **gender dysphoria.** While this is a very real issue, God doesn't make mistakes! Changing from what God made you goes totally against our Creator. This does not take away from the painful struggle that some people are going through, but God can always make a way for people to get free and His way is the only way to abundant life.

Many people struggling with gender dysphoria become suicidal. Not only from the battle in their minds but from being bullied and mistreated. This grieves my heart. We must see that while we may not understand their lifestyle, *hating, bullying or laughing at anyone* is reinforcing the lie to these people that they are not loved.

We should be loving to people identifying as someone they weren't born as. This is something that we should never laugh about or take lightly. We must show grace and compassion to everyone, just as God has shown it to us. But we cannot bend or change the truth! Speaking the truth in love will ultimately lead others to freedom!

Christians are being silenced in fear. When we speak out, or stand for what God says, we may be accused of being racists, bigots and haters. Basically, because we disagree with someone's lifestyle they may want to scare us into changing the truth by accusing us of hate. The enemy wants to silence the voice of God. God's way is the truth, and we must not be afraid to stand by the truth. This takes courage and bravery!

When a trans person changes their name they call their birth given name their "dead-name." Let's say a girl was born and her name was Anne. She began to "identify" as a boy. She starts to TRANSITION, or change her appearance and become a boy. She changes her name from Anne to Alex, and insists that she is now a he. The name Anne would be referred to as her dead-name.

I have read where people in the trans community do not ever want to be asked about or even referred to by their dead-name. It's as if they have killed off their former identity or the identity that God gave them. They have said their new name is the name they chose for themselves, which is true. I propose this is the enemy's counterfeit to the gospel.

Did you know that when you choose to follow Jesus, or invite Him into your heart, the old you dies. He takes all of your sinful nature and He nails it to the cross and it is dead and buried. You then TRANSITION into a new creation in Him. The old is gone and the new has come. The new you lives for what pleases God, not what pleases your flesh or your body. This is God's beautiful plan for your life. This is the gospel!

The enemy has distorted this desire in people's hearts and minds. Killing off your gender, changing your body, becoming who you say you should be, will never bring the peace and freedom that every heart desires. The only way is through Jesus. It's about who we become in Him, not who we become in this world. This is why if we cave to what the world is saying about being gay or transgender we are robbing people of the truth. The truth is exactly what people need to be set free.

There are many ways the enemy wants to deceive you about who you are and about your sexuality. The Bible tells us to run from sexual sin because it's sin that involves sinning against your own body.

1 Corinthians 6:19-20

Have you forgotten that your body is now the sacred temple of the Spirit of Holiness, who lives in you? You don't belong to yourself any longer, for the gift of God, the Holy Spirit lives inside your sanctuary. You were God's expensive purchase, paid for with tears of blood, so by all means, use your body to bring glory to God!

It is so beautiful that you can use your body to bring glory to God. Because of what Jesus did on the cross, sacrificing His life for yours, God's Holy Spirit dwells inside you. It feels so good to live in purity and in the light of the truth. It brings true joy and freedom to walk like Jesus and follow His ways.

God knew what He was doing when He designed you as a boy or a girl. He fashioned you perfectly in His image and it's only the enemy that distorts or wants to change that.

God designed sex and sexuality to be a wonderful gift between a married man and woman. Sex is something to be excited about and to look forward to in your life! God made you to desire physical pleasure in sex, but keeping it within the covenant of marriage is His plan. God would not have created this plan for purity if it was not possible for us to live out.

Philippians 2:13 NIV
> For it is God who works in you to will and act in order to fulfill his good purpose.

As you grow in relationship with Him, He will develop and mature and strengthen you. Your desires will merge into His. While you will still have sexual desires and feelings, they will change from pleasing your flesh or yourself and your body to pleasing Him. You will overcome the temptations to go outside of God's design for physical pleasure. **When you get physical pleasure it lasts for a moment, but pleasing God is the most fulfilling and gratifying way to live and lasts forever.**

God will help you manage your desires and He wants you to cast all of your troubles and struggles on Him, and let Him give you the strength in areas you are weak. The Bible says that apart from Him we can do nothing! You need His help in this area of your life. You can believe everything He says is true and want to follow Him and His ways but you MUST be in relationship with Him.

There is nothing God can't and doesn't forgive. He is the God of a million chances. He is most concerned with your heart and your life with Him. If you have experienced anything that you feel doesn't line up with God's desire for your life, He offers you love and forgiveness. If you focus on getting rid of the sin in your life, you may be consumed by it! I spent years trying to change my behavior to get to God, and it doesn't work. It seemed the harder I tried to change, the more I failed. Focus on your Heavenly Father, and He will work in your life to bring your wants and desires in line with His!

There are things we haven't discussed about sex, and as you get older you may hear things or see things that leave you with questions about what is true and what is right. You need to be free to ask questions to someone safe who you can trust, preferably a parent. You need to know what God says about things because His way will keep you the most protected, the most healthy, and the most free.

I pray you can connect with the heart of God regarding sex and your sexuality. I pray you can find friends that share in these values and can build you up and encourage you on the journey for purity. I pray that you will know the truth and that the truth will set you free from any unhealthy sexual history or patterns in your life. I pray you have a peace about the issue of sex and that you seek God on this issue and all issues, all the days of your life.

John 8:32 NIV
"Then you will know the truth, and the truth will set you free."

DISCUSSION
PARENTS AND LEADERS

- Offer note cards for questions to be written down at the beginning of discussion.
- Open the floor for any comments or questions.
- Answer the appropriate questions on note cards from the previous lesson and any new questions.

FAMILY OR GROUP

- Share if you know a family that looks different than the traditional family.
- Share ways you can show love to others who are in the homosexual or transgender lifestyle.
- Offer a safe way for anyone to share personal issues they may be struggling with.
- Read Psalm 139.

PRAYER

Thank You God for Your perfect love. Thank you God that You have all of the answers and that Your ways are the truth. Thank you God that just as Your word never changes, Your love for us never changes. Thank You Father, that You have good plans and purposes for our life, in our relationships, and in marriage. Thank You Father that anything we are tempted by or struggle with You have equipped us with your Holy Spirit who is our helper in all things. Thank You that we were made to be holy and righteous. Thank You that Your ways are the ways of peace, love, joy and everlasting life. Help us to be like You. In Jesus precious name, Amen.

10

DRUGS AND THE TREE OF LIFE

GATEWAYS, LIES AND THE GOOD STUFF

PARENTS AND LEADERS,

The statistics are scary. Drugs are destroying lives. If you haven't been affected by addiction, most likely you will. The enemy is stealing our youth by hooking them on drugs.

The goal of this chapter is to enlighten kids before they start experimenting with drugs and before habits and addictions set in. This lesson educates on different types of drugs, why some people use them, and the danger and fallout of addiction. I believe we can expose the lies the enemy uses to entice kids into using drugs. I believe we can build our kids up, communicate with them, pray with them and believe for a drug free life.

I have heard parents make excuses that kids are going to experiment or try things. Everything changes when a kid starts using drugs. Even if it is brief or recreational it can be dangerous. Ultimately, the risk of drug use can be life or death. I pray this lesson opens eyes to the dangers of drugs and brings resolve to hearts to stay away from things that can harm them.

Drugs and the Tree of Life
Gateways, Lies and the Good Stuff

When I was in 8th grade, well before the internet, I went to the library and checked out all of the books I could find on drugs. I wanted to teach kids my age about the dangers and harmful effects of drugs. Deep in my heart I had a passion to lead others towards good things and ultimately to God.

I began to study one of the books and was interested in learning more. I never, ever, ever thought that I would actually make a choice to use drugs, yet before I could finish my first book, I did.

I was against drugs, yet somehow I fell into a trap the enemy set for me. Why would I ever do something dangerous, bad for my body, harmful to my mind, against the law, against my parents, and what I knew was wrong?

The sneaky enemy preyed on me where I was weak. He knew that I wanted more than anything to fit in, to belong, to have friends, to be included. He knew that I wanted everyone to like me and I wanted to be important to my friends. He also knew I had this deep desire for more. I had a hunger in my heart for more than just the daily stuff going on around me. I had an appetite to be part of something exciting, something profound. I now know this wasn't all bad, but I went looking in the wrong places to satisfy those feelings and desires.

I had wounds in my heart. Pain and disappointment from my parents divorce and from my dad leaving when I was little. These were things I felt completely powerless to deal with. I was also comparing myself to everyone around me and I was coming up short, and I believed the lie that I was never going to be enough.

You should know, at the time, I didn't understand I was feeling all of these things. I can look back now and describe it to you. The point is, there were reasons I made some bad choices, but none of them are good enough to excuse what I opened myself up to.

One morning before school some kids that I thought were super cool, were in the gym in a group and it was obvious they were talking about something serious. My new boyfriend Ben, was there and he was talking to another girl and I was afraid he would like her more than me. When I joined them, they told me what they were talking about. She was going to get something called LSD and was selling it to anyone who wanted some. It was $5.00 and a few people were giving her money including Ben. I didn't know what LSD was, but figured it was a drug, and under pressure I chose to give her some money like the rest of the group. I wasn't planning to ever do LSD, but in the moment I wasn't worried about that. I had no idea the trouble I would be getting into or how that one quick and poor decision would alter the course of my life.

Before the day was over, multiple police arrived at the school with drug dogs and were searching lockers. I imagine in my locker they found my books on drugs but had no idea their purpose. I was pulled out of class and escorted to the counselor's office. Before stepping in, I saw Ben in another office and I knew what it was about. I had never been in trouble in my life and I had no idea how to handle what was about to happen. I can still remember the feeling of dread and fear. Although they never actually found drugs, I was kicked out of school and the story was being talked about throughout my community. It was in the newspaper and even the mayor was involved. I was banned from babysitting for many families I cared about. Most of my friends were no longer allowed to hang out with me. I wasn't invited to overnight parties anymore, and we even received *hate mail* describing what a horrible person I was.

The shock and pain of all of it, pushed me deeper into the belief, that I was not good enough. After a legal fight, we got accepted back in school. However, I had been branded, labeled, disgraced and humiliated. I began to believe what the world was saying about me, and the lies I was telling myself. Within a few months, I took LSD for real for the first time, and it was the scariest day of my life.

When I was offered the actual drug, I looked at it and thought, this tiny piece of paper could never hurt me. I had no idea what a lie that was. The piece of paper was smaller than my tiniest fingernail. **No matter how harmless, tiny, or innocent a drug...or the person offering the drug seems, one pill, one hit,** *one anything...can change everything.*

It seemed I had become a magnet for people who did drugs. Remember, you attract what you put out. If you feel worthless, you will attract others who feel the same way. Remember, what you believe about yourself, will come true if you don't let the truth override the lies.

I believe, when you use a substance that alters your mind, or the thoughts that you have, you are opening yourself up to the influence of the enemy in a dangerous way. I'm not talking about medicinal drugs used for healing purposes, I am talking about drugs used recreationally, or for fun or pleasure or to get high.

That day, I took LSD at about 7:00 in the morning. Within 30 minutes I had no idea where I was, who I was or what was happening. There was even a moment I forgot how to walk. I was terrified and trying hard to act normal because I knew if I got caught it would be serious. I can't describe what all was happening in my mind, but I can say I had no control of the thoughts and feelings I was having. At one point when the bell rang, I thought there was a tornado. I ended up failing a math test, and not being able to sleep for almost two nights. LSD is a very dangerous and powerful mind altering drug that can make you see and experience things that aren't real. LSD also is harmful to your body.

Even when your mind is sharp and clear there may be moments you have to battle to have good, healthy thoughts. How can you do this if you have opened the door for anything to come through your mind? You simply can't.

There are a lot of different drugs. They are ALL dangerous. Even the legal ones. Using any drugs that are not personally prescribed to you by your doctor is ILLEGAL. Or using any prescription drug in a way other than it was prescribed is also dangerous and illegal. Taking pills, smoking anything, using needles, snorting or sniffing, it doesn't matter which way you do it, you are causing harm to your mind, your body and your soul and anyone or anything that tells you differently is lying to you.

VAPING

Something that wasn't around when I was growing up is vaping. **Vaping** and using **e-cigarettes** has become an epidemic among teens. An epidemic is something that affects a large number of individuals within a population, community, or region at the same time. One reason for this, is that companies are marketing their e-cigarettes and vapes to kids and teens. They make vaping look cool, tasty and fun. Why? For money. Some kids believe that vaping isn't hurting them when in fact, vaping can harm your lungs, brain, heart and immune system according to the Center for Disease Control. They also have confirmed deaths from vaping and linked many serious vaping related lung injuries.

Juul has become very popular and looks like a flash drive. Often when I am walking around my neighborhood I find empty Juul pods on the street that someone, most likely teenagers, must have thrown out of the car window. That's how common it is for kids to use a Juul.

There are many different types of vapes and e-cigarettes. Unlike traditional smoking, vaping is easy to hide. E-cigarettes contain liquids that can have harmful chemicals in them and those chemicals become even more dangerous when they are heated. Most also have nicotine in them which is extremely addictive. **Nicotine** is the chemical agent in tobacco leaves that is stimulating to the brain. Often kids that vape end up smoking regular cigarettes, which are also addictive and even more harmful and proven to cause cancer.

Just because you don't immediately see or feel the harmful affects of something, doesn't mean it isn't doing damage to something inside of you. Many teens feel invincible, like nothing can or will hurt them, and that opens them up to risky behavior. The truth is, vaping isn't good for you and is very addictive.

Vaping has also been called a gateway drug. A **gateway** drug is simply a habit forming drug that can lead to the use of other, more addictive drugs. For example, if you are vaping and you feel like you are managing that, you are then prone to believing you can take on something a little riskier. Not only may you believe that, most likely you will try something else.

MARIJUANA

Marijuana has also been called a gateway drug. Marijuana is the most commonly used drug in America and often the first drug you or your friends will be offered, if you haven't already. Since it has become legal in some states, many teens and even adults argue that it is a safe drug to use. Not only is there scientific evidence that marijuana is harmful to a developing brain, there are many other issues that go along with using it.

Joints, blunts, bowls, bongs, pipes, and vapes are just some of the ways to smoke marijuana. Marijuana can be ingested and that means it can be sold or used in food. It can also be used in concentrated measures such as oils or waxes which may be more potent.

The ingredient in marijuana, a hemp based plant, that causes a high is THC. THC is a chemical that alters your mind. **"Getting high" means, creating an altered state of mind or conscious-**

ness. Science says the drug or chemical you use alters the cells throughout your body to cause euphoria.

Euphoria is a feeling or state of intense excitement, happiness or of well being or elation. While feeling euphoric sounds like a great thing, there are a multitude of side effects and problems that go with using drugs to achieve that feeling. Beyond the harmful effects on your body, using drugs has a huge impact on dopamine. Remember, dopamine is the natural chemical released in your brain in order to cause the pleasure feeling in the reward system. Doing drugs to get high releases large amounts of dopamine and now your brain is telling you to DO THAT AGAIN! Even if you think you are only going to try it once, you now have a message that's being signaled to you to get back to that feeling! In the case with some drugs, once you come off the feeling of being high, you have depleted or used up a lot of your natural dopamine and you may feel low or down without using drugs again.

Often teens experience a lot of heightened emotions and stress. Some teens have said they use marijuana to relieve stress. But there is a very dangerous problem with that. Not dealing with the issues you are facing, or the emotions you are feeling, only suppresses them. You are not learning how to cope, and those problems are still there. When teens begin to use drugs as an escape from reality, they are not learning how to deal with life, and they are causing even more problems for themselves down the road.

YOU ARE GIVING THE DRUG YOU ARE USING PERMISSION TO INFLUENCE OR CHANGE YOUR THOUGHTS

What often starts out as something people try out of curiosity, turns into a dependency or ultimately an addiction. I know a teenager who currently cannot handle the tiniest amount of disappointment or she goes over the edge unless she gets high.

She is no longer doing it for enjoyment, she admits she is doing it to cope and she hates herself for it, yet keeps doing it.

There are many adults that are in their 40's and 50's that have been using marijuana for years. I know some that still depend on marijuana to deal with stress or even minor things life throws their way. Adults dependent on marijuana often are people who have not advanced in their schooling, careers, families or faith. They lack ambition for life because when they get high they are content with just being high. Often they have all kinds of life problems piling upon and around them because they have yet to face reality.

In some states marijuana use is legal. In some states it is legal to use for medical purposes. People with chronic pain or certain diseases may benefit from the use of marijuana as prescribed by their doctor. That is totally different that using marijuana recreationally, or just to get high.

There are adults who use marijuana and appear to be functioning in their lives. I would argue that recreational use of any drug is not God's best for your life and keeps you from reaching your fullest potential

Often users suppress so many emotions and feelings that if they aren't high their anxiety starts to rise so they just keep getting high. Marijuana is addictive.

While some people who smoke marijuana or use other types of drugs, may get a euphoric feeling, others may get paranoid. **Paranoia** is delusions of persecution, or excessive or irrational suspicion and distrustfulness of others. An example of this would be; someone who is high, may believe someone is hiding in their bushes in front of their house and is going to kill them. Even though no one is there, and you are telling them no one is there, they may insist that someone is. They may even call the police and even go get a large knife out in order to protect themselves from something that isn't real. No matter what you say they don't believe you. Even when the police tell them no one is there, they don't believe them. This is a real example of an experience I witnessed with someone that was paranoid and delusional. You are taking a risk when you use drugs. You have no idea what can happen.

Another problem with drugs is that you have no idea what you are getting. While one day getting high may make you feel good, the next time you experience fear and paranoia and your heart rate is elevated and you are delusional, or believing things that are not real. There is no guarantee. **You can never trust a drug, or a person selling you one.** However, you can be sure that when people are getting high they want others to be with them because it makes them feel better about themselves and justifies their behavior.

Marijuana users argue that it isn't bad for you. While some people believe it is beneficial for medicinal purposes, science agrees it is bad for the brain that isn't fully developed, lowers IQ, causes memory problems, is harmful to your lungs, and is addictive. It is also true that getting high opens you up to other dangerous and risky behaviors because you aren't in a sober or clear mindset. Again, it is a gateway drug, if you think you can get away with this one, you may want to move on to something more. This is the vicious cycle with drugs.

Another epidemic that is sweeping our nation is **the abuse of prescription drugs.** Prescription opioids are drugs that doctors often prescribe for people suffering with pain, who have been injured or after surgeries. Painkillers like codeine, hydrocodone, morphine, oxycodone, and fentanyl are just a few. Klonopin, Xanax, Valium, and Ativan are other types of prescription drugs that people are abusing. They are often prescribed to treat stress, anxiety and panic attacks.

It is very important you get this. Never ever, ever, ever, take a pill that someone other than a doctor prescribes you. No matter what they say it is or isn't, don't do it. Even if kids at school are taking them, it doesn't change the facts. We can't even scratch the surface to understand the depths of darkness these drug addictions are causing. Again, no one starts out wanting to be an addict, but these types of drugs are so highly addictive, it doesn't take long and you may find yourself in a serious situation.

If you are prescribed a habit forming drug, be aware! This is how many people fall into the trap of drug addiction. I have seen families fall apart where a well meaning adult got addicted to a drug that was prescribed to them, began to abuse it, and couldn't stop.

These drugs are rampant in our schools and communities and while you may have not heard of them yet, most likely you will. Teens are using them for various reasons but very quickly an addiction can form. Not only do they change the chemicals in your brain, but the physical ramifications to your body can be just as serious. Not to mention, your heart.

Many pill addicts turn to **heroin** because heroin is cheaper and easier to get, even though it is illegal. Heroin is an opioid that gets someone high very fast.

When an addict doesn't get their fix, they will begin the symptoms of **withdrawal.** They may experience nausea, vomiting, rapid heart rate, intense cravings, muscle and bone aches, severe anxiety and panic, insomnia or being unable to sleep, muscle spasms, or seizures, JUST TO NAME A FEW WITHDRAWAL SYMPTOMS! Because of what they have done to the chemistry in their brain, they may experience severe depression where they literally cannot feel anything good unless they get drugs. This is why they keep doing the stuff over and over. As bad as this all sounds, I have heard detoxing from drug addiction is like hell on earth.

All of this may seem far out to you. Unfortunately as you grow and get older you will see just how dark the world of drugs and addiction can be. You may know someone personally, or know of someone who is addicted to drugs. If you do, you see how negatively it impacts their own life and their family.

Although I made some bad choices, I am thankful I didn't struggle with drug addiction. However, I witnessed the horrors of what it was doing to people I cared about. They wanted out, but they couldn't stop.

Ben ended up with an opiate addiction. He would battle and struggle to stop for years. He started with a regular marijuana habit, then he moved on to taking pills to get him high. When that wasn't enough, he would crush them and snort them. Eventually he was injecting drugs with needles. Eventually he wasn't even getting high anymore, just trying not to be sick from not having the drugs in his system. He would wake up each day and his mission was to score drugs, just to function. Eventually after a lot of rehab and detoxing he got free and clean. Even still every day he battled not using drugs. Then at the young age of 23, he relapsed, or fell back into his habit, and injected a lethal dose of heroin. He was driving his car when he passed out and wrecked and died.

When I met Ben, he was a kind and innocent kid with hopes and dreams. He was very smart, loved others and had a bright future ahead. Drugs stole his future and ultimately his life.

According to the National Institute on Drug Abuse, 130 people die every day in our country after overdosing on opioids, making it a public health crisis. They report that in 2017, more than 47,000 Americans died as a result of these drugs. They also say that in the same year 1.7 million people suffered from **substance abuse disorders** related to opioid use, and 652,000 suffered from a heroin use disorder. Can you even conceive of those numbers?

There are many other drugs that are abused to get high. Drugs such as **inhalants, cocaine, ecstasy, methamphetamines, cough syrups,** and the list goes on. While they come in various forms and give different types of highs, the problems with them are the same. Once you find yourself doing any of these, you have already entered a dangerous place where life and death is in the balance. Some of these drugs have killed people the very first time they have used them. Some of these, including LSD, have pushed people into committing suicide or murder out of a state of **delusion.** A majority of the reason our jails and prisons are full is because addicts have committed crimes either while high on drugs or in order to get high. When you hear stories of people doing awful crazy things, most often, drugs are involved.

Other common drugs being abused among teens, college kids and adults, are "focus drugs". Drugs such as **Vyvanse** and **Adderall.** Many people are prescribed these drugs to treat ADHD. The problem is, many people are misusing them with and without prescriptions. Adderall and drugs like it, are stimulants known to help concentration and focus. However, these drugs are an **amphetamine** which is highly addictive. When abused or misused these drugs are similar to that of **crystal meth, another deadly and addictive drug.** Side effects of Adderall abuse, or similar drugs are horrific.

Often people without a doctor's prescription, start taking Adderall to help them focus, study for a test, take an exam or work on a project. Initially, it seems to work really well. Studying for a test under the influence of Adderall may seem easier and it may feel good at first. When you get a good grade on the test it feels even better. So, now you are buying into the lie that you need Adderall to help you study, make good grades, or just get things done. So you start taking it regularly but you justify it because it is for your grades or to help you be productive. It doesn't take long and the effects aren't working like they did at first because you have built up a tolerance to it. Your brain is sending you a signal to get back to that higher level of dopamine and so in order to do so you increase your dosage or you take more pills. Instead of taking 1 Adderall now you are taking 2. Before long you will need to take 3 to achieve the same results. Taking Adderall can make you feel alive and energetic and focused. Until it wears off. Then you may feel down, sad and depressed or even hopeless...until you get more. This abuse cycle is happening everywhere.

Some people without a prescription, have tried Adderall and had a very bad experience. Adderall increases your heart rate and this can cause severe anxiety and panic. I knew a teen that believed he was having a heart attack and ended up in the emergency room after his first time taking Adderall. He said he was taking it to focus in school, but it scared him so much he will never take it again. You never know how any drug will affect you compared to the next person.

Many people are prescribed focus drugs for a reason. If that is you, just follow what your doctor says and don't share your medication with your friends. Doctors are responsible for prescribing the right dose of medication based on many factors. If a doctor has not prescribed something to you, you should never take it.

Drug induced psychosis or extreme paranoia is a side effect of abusing Adderall and other similar drugs. One of my friends, Sarah, had a severe Adderall addiction. When she would get her prescription filled she would binge on the pills or take them all over a period of days, until they were gone. She wouldn't sleep for days and she would pick at her face so bad that she had holes, sores and scabs all over it. She would get in an extreme psychotic state of mind where no one could reason with her. She called me one night and told me a plane had crashed near her house and the police were trying to cover it up. None of that was true but I couldn't reason with her. She would get angry if I tried to suggest she was delusional and nothing I said would convince her of what was truly going on. She would drive her little children around saying someone was following them for hours. She always thought people were spying on her and out to get her. She lived in torment while she was abusing drugs, and then she would run out of drugs and go through painful withdrawal and severe depression. She would be in the pit of despair unless she took some other drug to try to function. Then the time would come for her to get her prescription filled again, and she would start the cycle over.

Sarah was so addicted to drugs that she took them while she was pregnant. When one of her babies was born, he was born an addict. To watch an infant go through the torment of drug withdrawal is excruciating and babies are being born addicted to drugs at alarming rates.

Sarah was a precious and sweet girl who adored children. She had a big beautiful smile and loved people. She is someone I love and care about and was very close to when we were young. Over time she started to change and act different, but would never tell the truth about her drug addiction. Even when her son was born addicted, she would not admit she was taking pills. I watched a healthy, happy person turn into a tormented, paranoid, woman with mental illness. I tried to help her, but she shut me and so many others out of her life. Adderall addiction stole almost everything from her.

Many people addicted to drugs don't even know they are. That's how deceptive drugs can be. Many addicts neglect their families, or even their own kids, because they are solely focused on getting high. All they can see is their next high and when they get that one, they are already worrying about how they are going to get the next one. Remember how we described the signal your brain sends when you are in the trap of addiction? It's like someone tapping on your shoulder and never stopping. Tap, tap, tap, tap, tap, tap, tap. The only thing that makes it stop is a hit or a pill or the next high. Then soon it starts again.

When you take, or smoke, or inhale, or ingest, or snort, or shoot up a drug, you are giving away your ability to control your own thoughts, or feelings or even actions. You are giving an element of power to whatever comes in or out of your mind, body and soul. It may feel good for a minute, it may make you laugh, it may give you a shot of excitement or it may make you feel like you are on top of the world. It may make you feel like you are the best looking, or the strongest person around. But it will leave you as fast as it came with more chaos and confusion and feelings of despair. It will leave you wanting that feeling again, and again, and again, and without realizing it, you may become an addict.

The people you hang around will determine so much of your life! When my friend group started to change, I started to change. While I was a rule follower, and had a heart to do what was right, I was very much influenced by the pressure of people around me. I wanted to fit in and was willing to do dangerous or unhealthy things in order to do so. I did what I knew was wrong in my heart. When I did my first drug, smoked my first cigarette, had my first sip of alcohol, I had to push down the guilt and the conviction God had placed in my heart, what is in all of our hearts.

Romans 1:19

In reality, the truth of God is known instinctively, for God has embedded this knowledge inside every human heart.

We know right from wrong no matter what excuses we make. No matter what is going on in our lives, we know.

Drugs can be scary and dangerous and even deadly yet they can be very seductive. **Seductive means, tempting, attractive or enticing.** Drugs can be captivating, charming, fascinating, provocative, and inviting. Drugs themselves are a lie. They are not what they present themselves to be. There are people that will tell you about "good" things drugs can do for you. You need to know, there is nothing good about abusing drugs.

TWO TREES IN THE GARDEN

It's much like when Eve ate from the bad tree in the garden. That tree must have been so beautiful. Yet she knew in her heart to eat from it was wrong. She listened to the seductive alluring voice of the enemy and allowed herself to be convinced.

Unfortunately, you are going to be tempted. It may sound crazy now, but you will hear of people you know, using drugs, or maybe even your friends. It will become more common to you as you get older. You may find yourself in a situation where you are surrounded by people who are using drugs or you are being asked if you want some. It is easier than you may think to be influenced, and that is why it is important that you prepare yourself for these moments as best as you can. If you find yourself in a tempting situation, I pray you remember the truth.

THE MORE YOU MAKE A GOOD CHOICE THE EASIER IT BECOMES.

THE MORE YOU MAKE A BAD CHOICE, THE HARDER IT BECOMES TO MAKE A GOOD CHOICE.

Facing your problems, and the pressures life is throwing at you is one way you can be on top of temptation. Talk to trusted friends or family, talk to God. Dealing with your disappointments or the pain in your life, will keep your heart guarded from the enemy.

If you are already using drugs occasionally or in the battle of being addicted to them, my prayer is that you would allow the truth of God to shine on your heart. It is no coincidence you are here now and there is no doubt that with God you can overcome anything. My prayer for you is that God would lead you to the right person to help you out of the tangled web you are in. Just know, any amount of drug use is a problem.

I have tried to help multiple people out of drug addiction and failed. When someone is using drugs or under the influence, it is almost impossible to convince them they need to stop or need help. The longer someone uses drugs the more they change. They withdraw from people that love them and their lives become secretive. Often they lie and steal and do things they would have never done before because they are totally consumed with their habit. People on drugs are the only ones that can make the choice to stop.

There was another tree in the garden and it was the most beautiful. The tree of life. We still have a choice what tree we want to eat from, so to speak. The tree that God wants for us to choose is filled with the fruit of the Spirit and it brings life. The other tree, the one that Satan wants to tempt us with, is the counterfeit to that. Counterfeit means, *made with imitation of something else, made with intent to deceive.*

The enemy is a copycat, and he is still trying to be like God. I think of drugs like the counterfeit to the fruit of the Spirit. Drugs dress themselves in so-called peace and love, yet bring chaos and darkness. Drugs whisper that you can be *better,* or *smarter,* or *happier,* yet they attack your self worth, bring confusion to your mind, and leave you in despair. Drugs lie that you are escaping your problems, when you are actually bringing on more. Drugs seem to offer you an instant solution, but they ensnare you into a world where you feel trapped in hopelessness.

Galatians 5:22 NIV

But the fruit of the Spirit is love, joy, peace, forbearance, kindness, goodness, faithfulness, gentleness, and self-control. Against such things there is no law.

We can eat from the wrong tree, or be led by the world and our fleshly desires. When we do that, we may reap stress, anxiety, fear, anger, impatience, lack of self control, depression, and even hate. **We can be led by the Spirit, and we can have limitless access to what God has to offer.**

The result of His presence within us is love, joy that overflows, inner peace, the ability to be patient, showing kindness, doing good things, having a gentle heart, and being able to control our emotions and feelings, no matter what is happening around us.

MADE FOR MORE

I knew I was made for more than an ordinary life, yet I didn't understand the hunger in my heart. I had an appetite inside of me for bigger and better things than the mundane. Thank God He protected me and redeemed me from my bad choices, but I learned through some hard experiences that anything outside of God would not satisfy that desire. I have learned that nothing compares to being filled by Him. Nothing touches *being in the presence of the real and living God who will pour out joy in a way that no drug can come close to.* God's goodness and love is pure and holy and fulfilling. It's actually beyond fulfilling, It's impossible to contain.

God has taken all of my bad choices and failures and used them for my good, and I delight in giving Him glory. I may have been derailed from the path I should have taken, but He never left me. Here I am all of these years later, doing just what He put in my heart. I am finally able to tell others of the dangers of drugs and even better, I can tell of the goodness of God.

If there is anything in your life that you are hiding from the people that love you, that is a huge indicator that there is an area the enemy has a stronghold on you. The very thing you are hiding is the thing that you need to tell someone.

If you are afraid to tell because you don't want to stop, or disappoint people you love, you need to pray. Speak out loud to God, and ask Him for the courage to do what you know you need to do. Ask Him to show you the right person and act fast. This is an opportunity to get free from whatever it is!

God has given us everything we need and more in this life. We all make mistakes, wrong choices, have struggles, disappointments and setbacks. When we face challenges it is important that we face them, even if it doesn't seem easy. It's how we deal with those things that transforms us into being like Jesus. It's bringing Him into all of it when we overcome.

God has given us access to everything He has, if we just seek Him. Beyond just dealing with the hard issues life throws at you, you were made for more. You were made to experience things that are out of this world good, the supernatural peace that God gives and exuberant joy from your Father and Creator. You were made to make a difference on this earth and to bring others into the Kingdom.

Proverbs 11:30 NIV

The fruit of the righteous is a tree of life, and the one who is wise saves lives.

DISCUSSION
PARENTS AND LEADERS

- Ask for feedback or questions from the lesson. Ask what are their thoughts about drugs. Have them share or write them down.
- Ask if they have heard of any of these drugs in particular or know anyone that is using them.
- Share any personal stories about how drug addiction has affected your life. Example: maybe from a family member or friend.

KIDS AND GROUP

- Share how common it is for kids to vape or use any drugs where you go to school or in your neighborhood.
- Think about a friend group or places you go that may influence you to do something you know is harmful.
- Write a prayer, sharing your heart with God about drugs, and ask Him to protect you from the trap of drugs. Ask Him to speak to your heart about how He

feels about you and How He wants you to protect your mind and body. Write down what you believe He is saying.

- Speak this over your group or family

Psalm 46

God is our refuge and strength, an ever present help in trouble.

Therefore we will not fear, though the earth give way and the mountains fall into the heart of the sea, though its waters roar and foam and the mountains quake with their surging.

There is a river whose streams make glad the city of God, the holy place where the Most High dwells.

God is within her, she will not fall; God will help her at the break of day.

Nations are in uproar, kingdoms fall; he lifts his voice, the earth melts.

The Lord Almighty is with us; the God of Jacob is our fortress.

Come and see what the Lord has done, the desolations he has brought on the earth.

He makes wars cease to the ends of the earth.

He breaks the bow and shatters the spear; he burns the shields with fire.

He says, "Be still, and know that I am God; I will be exalted among the nations, I will be exalted in the earth." The Lord Almighty is with us; the God of Jacob is our fortress.

PRAYER

Father, thank You that You have given us everything we need in this life. Thank You that you have equipped us to overcome challenges and struggles we may face. Thank You for your Holy Spirit who lives inside of us and can always lead, guide and comfort us. Thank You that

Your desire is for us to be sober minded and sharp so that we can rest in Your peace, love and comfort no matter what we are faced with. Thank You that even when we stumble and fall and get off track You use those things to transform us, when we bring everything to You. Help us to see the trap of drugs for what it is. Help us to be on guard for the enemy's plan to get us down the wrong path. We ask you to bring the right friends to us so that we can have the support and encouragement in making wise choices for our lives. Thank You that You have made us for more. Thank You that You made us to live a supernatural life that is exciting and meaningful and filled with purpose. Wake us up to those great things that You have called us to. Thank you Lord that You are enough. In Jesus name, Amen.

11

ALCOHOL AND GUARDING YOUR HEART

UNDERAGE DRINKING, EFFECTS AND A CLEAR MIND

PARENTS AND LEADERS,

Regardless of the age of your children, it is a good time to start a discussion about alcohol and safety. It is a good time to think and pray about where you stand with your children drinking. Often parents allow their underage children to drink because they believe that is a better option than to be in the dark. Other parents have a zero tolerance policy. Where do you stand?

Start the dialogue with your spouse and your children about what the consequences will be if your children are drinking underage.

Either way, our kids need to be educated on the dangers of alcohol. We need to be clear with them about what our expectations are, and when they make mistakes, they need to know we are a safe place to come.

Perhaps it is most important that we are modeling healthy behavior in our own drinking.

Alcohol and Guarding Your Heart
Underage Drinking, Effects and a Clear Mind

As you grow up, you will be faced with the temptation of drinking alcohol underage. Most people frown upon people abusing drugs, however, drinking alcohol is pretty accepted in our culture, but can be a serious problem.

Beer, wine, and liquor or mixed drinks, are types of alcoholic drinks. It is very common for underage kids to drink alcohol, even though the legal drinking age in the United States is 21 years old. Many adults drink alcohol, and that is one reason it is easy for kids to have access to it.

I have never heard of a kid that actually liked the way alcohol tastes when they first tried it. I believe God put that instinct in kids for a reason. Typically, the smell, sight or taste of alcohol does not attract kids and that is because it can harm them.

Alcohol can be extremely dangerous for anyone, especially when you are under 21. There are many reasons there is a legal drinking age. The effects of alcohol on a young person are much stronger than an adult. Also, as I have said, your brain isn't fully developed until age 25. That means, your decision making skills aren't fully formed, and being under the influence of alcohol can lead you to make bad decisions as well as be harmful to your brain and body.

Some adults drink alcohol because they like the taste of it. Alcohol is also something some adults enjoy socially or with friends. Many adults drink alcohol to relax after a long day or on the weekends or on vacation. As long as adults are responsible and not drinking too much, drinking alcohol is a personal decision. Many adults know the effects of alcohol and how to be safe when drinking. Many don't. **Controlling the amount of alcohol you consume can be difficult, even for adults.** Abusing alcohol or drinking too much can have a negative impact on families and have serious consequences.

UNDERAGE DRINKING

Kids drink alcohol for many of the same reasons that kids do drugs. Often it's because other kids are doing it. **Peer pressure is the influence you feel from others to do something you otherwise would not do.** If you are in a group of people that start drinking, you may feel pressured to also drink, even if you don't want to. Or let's say you go to a party where someone has snuck alcohol and all of your friends are trying it. When it's your turn to drink, you don't want to look weak or stand out. You want to fit in and be a part of what everyone is doing. That's peer pressure, and it happens all of the time.

Everyone wants to be accepted and not outcast or made to feel different. The fear of being laughed at or made fun of is part of peer pressure.

Often, kids are just curious about alcohol and that is a reason they try it. Many kids have seen their parents drink and they want to see what it's like. Adults drinking versus kid's underage drinking, are two very different things.

EFFECTS OF ALCOHOL

Let's say, Sally is drinking beer. Alcohol enters her bloodstream, and it starts to travel around her body. About 10 minutes after she starts drinking, she may start to feel the effects of the alcohol and ultimately it slows down the way her body functions. Eventually, the alcohol is carried throughout all of the organs in her body. Sally's body will begin to try and break down or rid itself of the alcohol. If she is drinking more alcohol than her body can break down, she will begin feeling drunk.

Each one of us may respond differently to alcohol. Your age, your body type, how much food you have eaten, whether you are a boy or girl, how quickly you drank the alcohol and how often you drink will determine how alcohol affects you. The same amount of alcohol can affect you differently on different days.

Let's say Sally is drinking too much alcohol. The first thing that may happen is she starts to slur her speech. Basically she sounds like her tongue is thicker than normal. She may be more talkative or seem more self-confident. If she continues to drink, she may start laughing more than usual, or she may feel really sad and start crying or getting upset for what seems like no reason. She may have a hard time walking or standing straight. She also may get angry or mad over nothing. Often when people are drunk they forget what just happened and they may repeat themselves over and over. Getting drunk will always result in you acting different. When you get drunk you lose self-control.

Many people have been hurt from falling down while they are drunk. With your impulses being slowed down, normal activities can be dangerous when someone is under the influence. Many people have drowned when they were drunk. Often people get into physical fights with others that they wouldn't normally have gotten into. A lot of crazy things happen when people are drunk!

When someone drinks too much alcohol they are left with what is called a **hangover**. Often it happens the next day, but once the alcohol leaves your system you may feel sick. You may have a headache, diarrhea or you may be nauseous like the way you feel when you have had a stomach bug. Some people will actually be throwing up. Each person is different but you may feel like this for the entire next day or until your body recovers.

The amount of alcohol present in someone's blood is called their blood alcohol level. There is a legal amount of alcohol adults are allowed to have and still be able to drive. If an adult goes over that amount and gets caught by the police they will get arrested for a DUI, or Driving Under the Influence. Getting a DUI is very serious. You will go to jail for driving under the influence of alcohol. You will have to go to court. You will also lose your driver's license for a period of time, and a DUI will cost thousands of dollars. You may get fired from your job. You will also have a record, where anyone can see that you have committed a crime. From that point forward in your life, your record will show the charge of drinking and driving against you. You may be able to Google your name and have it show that you have been arrested for driving under the influence of alcohol. Beyond all of that, you will have risked driving impaired or intoxicated where you could have harmed yourself or others.

Drinking too much alcohol can make you not care about yourself or others.

Drinking too much can cause risky behavior. My friend in college jumped off the roof of a 2 story house into a little swimming pool. He hit the side of the pool and it busted the pool and water rushed underneath him. The water that rushed underneath him may have saved his life. He could have broken his legs, been paralyzed, or worse. Normally he would have never done that!

Drinking alcohol may cause you to use poor judgment. Because you have lost self-control and your ability to make good decisions, you may make some really bad ones. While under the influence of alcohol you may be more likely to try other drugs. Research proves that you will be much more likely to have sex if you are under the influence of alcohol. You are also likely to put yourself in a dangerous position to be taken advantage of sexually. When you drink alcohol you let down boundaries that you might normally have set.

BINGE DRINKING is when someone drinks a lot in a short period of time. Four or five drinks within two hours would be considered binge drinking. When someone has had so much alcohol that their body can't break it down they get very sick. Vomiting, passing out or slower breathing are resultless of binge drinking. Unfortunately most kids that drink, binge drink.

Another risk of drinking too much alcohol is what is called **blacking out.** This is when someone may appear to be alert and interacting with others but they have no idea what is going on or no memory of what has happened. They may end up passing out and when they wake up the next day have no idea what went on after they began drinking. Blacking out is common and is very dangerous. Blacking out leaves a person vulnerable to getting hurt, or hurting others.

Drinking too much alcohol may cause you to do embarrassing things. Because you lose self-control, you don't realize you are behaving silly or inappropriate. While kids often drink to be "cool," other kids will quickly make fun of them for acting drunk or doing stupid things while they are drinking. People who are drunk do stupid things, especially kids.

Alcohol poisoning is when someone gets so sick from drinking too much alcohol too fast that they need to go to the hospital or they could die.

Moderating, or controlling, how much alcohol you drink can be very difficult for adults, so the younger you are the more difficult and often impossible it is.

ALCOHOL ADDICTION

Just like drugs, alcohol is addictive. Alcohol may even be more addictive because it is easier to get, and cheaper than most drugs. Just like drugs trigger the reward system in your brain, the same thing happens when you drink alcohol. Often people like to drink alcohol because it seems to momentarily take their cares away, loosen them up or make them feel like they don't care. There is always a downside to using any substance to make you "feel" happy. It won't last, unless you get more of what made you feel that way. This is how the enemy hooks you into a habit or an addiction to alcohol.

Often when someone gets in a habit of drinking alcohol, it can have a way of making a normal day or night without alcohol difficult or boring. Because alcohol can initially put you in a good mood, and make you feel excited when it first starts to affect you, you may find yourself drawn to doing it again and again. The problem is, this is how people become dependent on alcohol. It is very important that we are able to enjoy our life without any substances. This is also important for our relationship with God.

While God is not a *big bad rules* God, He warns us in His word about getting drunk. He knows how harmful alcohol can be and that we can miss out on things from Him if we are foggy minded or intoxicated.

Sadly, alcohol addiction has destroyed many lives. Alcohol is the reason many kids have been abused, many divorces have happened and the reason many people have died.

I know of a nice successful man who loved his family. He was always involved with his kid's sports and activities, but he would go home each day and drink beer, a good bit of it. As the years passed he found himself drinking beer when he first woke up in the morning. Eventually he left his entire family and lived in random places so that he could stay drunk. His family still loved him, but they suffered a lot from the bad choices he made. He ultimately got very sick from the effects of all the alcohol and he died. It was a tragic way to see a great life end.

This is not to scare you. This is real life stuff. Many people can maintain an addiction or get away with it for awhile but ultimately it catches up with them. In my family line, alcohol has destroyed lives. My grandfather, was drunk and passed out in his chair while smoking a cigarette and caught his house on fire. He was not a bad man, but the effects of his drinking damaged his children severely. When he was sober he was loving and kind, but he was a very mean drunk. His children suffer to this day from the mean things he did while drinking.

While the world celebrates and normalizes getting drunk, it doesn't bring true joy. The enemy wants to hook kids and teens into drinking so that they will make poor choices and dangerous decisions. The truth of God is much stronger than any lie the enemy can ever tell.

Proverbs 23:31- 34

And don't be drunk with wine, but be known as one who enjoys the company of the lovers of God. For drunkenness brings the sting of a serpent, like the fangs of a viper spreading poison into you soul. It will make you hallucinate, mumble, and speak words that are perverse. You'll be like a seasick sailor being tossed to and fro, dizzy and out of your mind. You'll wake only to say, "What hit me? I feel like I've been run over by a truck!" Yet off you'll go, looking for another drink!

Through scripture, God is giving us a clear description. He compares being drunk with being bitten by a poisonous snake where the venom runs through your body into your soul. Alcohol can cause you to mumble and say perverse things that are inappropriate or even sexually perverted. Being drunk causes you to stumble around, be out of your mind only to wake up, be totally hungover and sick, and then to go off and look for another drink. That sounds crazy, but is literally what people struggling with alcohol addiction do.

God loves you so much. He wants you to love yourself and care for yourself and for your body. Drinking alcohol while you are underage, is dangerous and illegal and can get you into a lot of trouble. It is also abusive to your own body.

Choosing to do things that are against the law, against your parents or against God, brings stress and anxiety to your life. Lying to the people that love you makes you feel bad inside. Choosing to do what we know is wrong has consequences. You may not see them or feel them at first, but eventually you may have deep regret.

I believe God is raising up young kids who are going to follow Him down a path of righteousness. I think these kids are going to be so strong in their walk with God that they will be teaching many adults what He is like. I think it will be easy for many of you to make wise choices because your main concern will be your relationship with your Heavenly Father. The reward will be so great.

If you have a problem with alcohol, you are loved. If someone you love has a problem with alcohol, they are loved. There is nothing too big for God to heal and restore. He can take any hurt or broken person and make them like new. He can wash away all of your mistakes and sins and darkness in one moment of surrender. I pray you find the right people to help you. I pray for your loved one, and you can too. God is so good, and if you ask Him and believe, He will come to the rescue.

DISCUSSION
PARENTS AND LEADERS

- Ask your children or group to share their thoughts and feelings about alcohol.
- Share any family history with alcoholism.
- Share any personal stories about people who have been affected by alcohol (car accidents, legal trouble, divorce.)
- Share how you feel about alcohol and how you make choices to be responsible with it.
- Explain to your child or group how they can always come to you, or another safe adult, if they drink alcohol and need help. It is never too early to say this.
- Parents, if you think the timing is appropriate, explain what your expectations are and the consequences your children will face it they drink underage.
- Encourage your children or group to support each other when they are faced with a situation of underage drinking.

FAMILY AND GROUP

- Share ways you can help deal with peer pressure.
- Example: change the subject when it comes up, don't go where it is or leave the situation, have support from friends that support your choice not to drink

Memorize this scripture or write it in your journal.

1 Peter 5:8-9

Be alert and of sober mind. Your enemy, the devil, prowls around like a roaring lion looking for someone to devour. Resist him, standing firm in the faith, because you know that the family of believers throughout the world is undergoing the same kind of suffering.

PRAYER

Thank You Father for giving us a sober mind. Thank You for your protection from the enemy. Thank You that we have a direct connection to You. Thank You for the fruit of self-control. Shine Your light on all of our ways that don't belong. Highlight the truth in our hearts to know what it means to be sober and clear. Give us wisdom and strength to make wise choices regarding alcohol. Draw others to us that can stand with us in righteousness. In Jesus name, Amen.

12

WALKING WITH GOD

FAITH, WORSHIP AND THANKSGIVING

PARENTS AND LEADERS,

Sometimes as adults we are desensitized to the voice of God. Often our kids faith is stronger than our own and they hear Him more than we do. I pray when your kids share ways they believe they hear from God, you can support them and build them up, without getting theological. Often we theologize our way right out of the truth. This lesson is light and easy and I pray it blesses you.

Walking with God
Faith, Worship and Thanksgiving

I believe God wants to walk with you like He walked with Adam and Eve in the garden. When sin came into the world, that wasn't possible, but because of Jesus, we are made perfect before God. That means, no matter what is happening in our lives, good or bad, we have access to Him, when we believe.

FAITH

Believing *in* God is great, but remember, the enemy even believes in God. There is much more than believing *in* Him. As we get to know Him, Faith is *believing Him,* no matter what we are feeling, no matter what is going on around us.

In the Bible book of Hebrews, there are some great examples of people who heard from God, and stepped out and believed for something huge. The natural mind would say they were crazy, but they knew God, and because of their faith, they changed the world.

Imagine, Noah was building the biggest boat ever made when there was no sign of a flood. This took him a long time, and it made no sense to people. He knew God, He listened to God, and it saved his entire family, and the animals too.

The difference in people who live their lives believing *in* God and those who *believe* God is **relationship.** People who have a relationship with God, live their lives on earth as those who belong to another realm, which would be heaven.

As far back as I can remember, I have wanted to have a baby. I believed that was one of the main reasons I was on earth. I felt like I wanted this more than any person in the world. I dreamed about the day I would have my very own baby. One day when I was sitting on the porch in the sunshine, I heard the voice of God speak to my heart. He said, *"you will have a daughter and her name will be Dylan."* It was so exciting, I wanted to have her that day! But God knew that we were about to face many challenges in order to have a baby. Eventually, a doctor said "it is impossible for you to get pregnant and have a baby, it will never happen." The doctor said there was no way ever. But I was believing what God said!

Luke 1:37

Not one promise from God is empty of power, for nothing is impossible with God!

I knew God was the one that put that dream and desire in my heart. I stood on His promise for a daughter. I knew what was real or true in heaven, needed to become reality on earth.

God knew our journey to have a baby would be hard at times. He knew there would be struggles and disappointment. I remember one of those times well. I was at a friends house with four other women that were pregnant, and they were all younger than me. They were talking about how excited they were and all of the joys I wanted to experience.

The enemy tried to tell me it would never happen for me, and if I based my belief on what things looked like, I could have believed him. He tried to get me to be bitter and angry and discouraged. After being surrounded by those pregnant friends, God moved my heart to humble myself, celebrate for them, pray for them and be happy for them. God turned a difficult situation into something powerful for me. He used a hard time in my life to teach me more about His ways, to grow me and change me.

God had a bigger plan in mind than me just getting what I wanted. I chose each day to get up and believe. I stood on the promise He gave me, no matter how hard things were. My walk with God became stronger than ever before, because I had to depend on Him for what I wanted.

Hebrews 11:1 NIV

Now faith is the confidence in what we hope for and assurance about what we do not see.

I longed for a baby. I had to be certain of what I hoped for even though it didn't appear it was going to happen. I knew that with God, ANYTHING IS POSSIBLE! No matter what the doctor said! I knew if it wasn't God's will for my life, He would change my heart.

Spending time with God strengthened my faith. I found a Bible verse that I chose to hold onto and believe.

Psalm 37:4 NIV
Delight yourself in the Lord, and He will give you the desires of your heart.

God knows the desires of your heart in every season. You may be searching for good friends, or you may be hoping to make the baseball team, or cheerleading. You may want to be an artist or a musician. You may want to start your own company or maybe go to the moon. You may not know yet exactly what you want in life, but you were made for great things. No matter what you are dreaming about or hoping for, when you delight in the Lord, He will take you on a journey to give you the desire of your heart!

There will be times you are let down. Everything will not always go your way. But if you stick with God, even when things are tough, you will be ok! Keep delighting in Him, by learning more and more about His nature and His goodness.

We were ecstatic when we got pregnant, and we thought for sure it was our girl Dylan. A few days before we went to see the ultrasound to know for certain, God spoke to my heart again and I heard the name Rivers. It changed everything! I knew the baby in my belly was a boy, and I knew that God had given me the best gift and surprise! And I was right!

People told me, this may be the only time you get pregnant, you should just name your son Dylan, but I knew that was not what God said, and I chose to have faith and believe that He had more children for me in my future.

Once I had that real baby in my arms, God showed me very clearly, that little Rivers was the desire of my heart. God knew better than me what I was hoping for! That little boy exceeded everything I could have ever dreamed of, and still does.

A little over 3 years later, baby Dylan was in my belly. There was a time when her life was in danger but I remembered the promise God had given me. Even though I went through some scary things I trusted God and she was born healthy. She is a promise from heaven and her life is marked with love and joy. God knew her well before she was in my womb and He knows all of the days of her life, just like He knows yours.

When you have faith and believe and trust God, miracles happen. Doctors are awesome and we need them. We used a lot of medicine to help us get pregnant, but God is bigger than any limitation, sickness or setback. Not only that, God is good, and He wants you to have your hearts desire! After all, He is the one that put them there.

DELIGHTING IN THE LORD MEANS BEING HIS FRIEND

When you have faith that God wants a relationship with you, it is easy and wonderful to walk with Him. He is ALWAYS with you and you are always in His presence. Sometimes you feel it, sometimes you don't. When you don't feel it, *have faith.*

God's desire is that you would know Him. How do you get to know someone? By spending time with them. That means giving some of your day to talking to him, or praying. Do you have to be in a good mood, say things the right way, or have made no mistakes that day? No! What He wants is for you to open your heart to Him, not by cleaning up your act, but by being real with Him.

With most of our friends we don't try and get all perfect before we hang with them. Not only do we want to share things going on in our lives with our friends, we want to hear about them too. Having a relationship with God is like this.

PRAYER

There are a lot of great things you can learn about prayer. I get distracted very easy so it helps me to sometimes write my prayers in a journal. It's also cool to look back at them and see the ways God has answered me. There are times of deep quiet prayer. I have times I need to be alone so I can pray out loud. While we can always grow in our prayer life, the most important thing you need to know is, JUST DO IT. While there may always be better ways to pray, there is no wrong way to pray, and do it night and day!

As you get to know God, if you give Him time and space you will hear from Him. Not only do I write my prayers, but I often write what I believe God is speaking to my heart.

GOD SPEAKS TO US

Sometimes people have literally heard God's voice. This has never happened to me. I have heard God in my heart. I can't explain it, but I knew it was Him. It wasn't my thought, it wasn't the enemy's thought, it was God.

God's voice is always true. His words are perfect and alive. God's voice brings understanding or sheds light on something. When God speaks it is often wrapped in kindness, joy, love and peace. There is no darkness or confusion in God's voice.

Sometimes His voice is gentle and quiet, and sometimes a thought just pops in your head and it will bring hope, excitement or joy in your heart.

God can speak to you with a sign. Rainbows are a sign God uses to remind us of His promise. When I see a rainbow, I believe it is God speaking. Sometimes a butterfly, a lady bug, a shooting star or a mountain will speak to our hearts. They could show up at just the right moment and you know it is Him and you know what message He is personally sending you.

God can speak to you in your dreams. Sometimes it's hard to know for sure, but there have been times when I just knew I had a dream that came from God.

There are times when God may speak to you through numbers. For several months I was seeing the number 1832 everywhere. I would see it on license tags, on TV or in random places. It seemed like twice a day I would glance at the time and it was 8:32. I felt like God was highlighting those numbers. It was like a fun mystery to me.

One morning I was praying and asking God what it meant and I believe He lead me to a certain part of the Bible for the answer. Through scripture He was confirming something I had been contemplating and suddenly it made total sense. It was so cool to understand that scripture and to know that God sees me! God sees you! And when He speaks to you it's so awesome.

Although we don't base everything on our feelings, there are times you may just feel like God is telling you to do something, or maybe He is telling you not to. The important thing is that you open your heart to hear from Him.

One way you can know you are hearing from God is through the Bible. God will never say anything to you that doesn't align with scripture. When you read your Bible sometimes you may feel you are just reading. Sometimes you will know God is giving you understanding of something. The more I read the Bible the more I know when I'm hearing from Him.

Sometimes, I will just hear a verse and I know He is saying something to me. I will look it up and I am always amazed how it was exactly what I needed. Often when I am talking to a friend and they are sharing a problem with me, I will hear a scripture and I know it is a message from God to them.

If you need direction on where to go in the Bible, you can always start by reading Psalms. Find a Psalm that is speaking your heart, and read it over and over, and meditate on it. It may be hard to understand at first, but the more you read, the more God will reveal Himself to you by His spirit. It's truly the most amazing thing and it goes beyond your mind right to your spirit.

In any situation I can pray and I can even ask God questions. I can wait and listen and be expectant for an answer. Often the answer is the first thing that pops in your mind. It may not be, but it's ok to try it out. If I am in a difficult situation I may ask the Holy Spirit what to say or what to do and I wait to hear.

WHAT IF I GET IT WRONG?

Ha! God loves you and me, He will not be mad if we get something wrong that we think He is saying. There are ways we can know it's Him and this can take practice and discernment. The worst thing we can do is not listen for God to speak because we are afraid of getting it wrong. Then we are shutting ourselves off from His voice. Not cool!

God never speaks to you through a spirit of fear. It's always lining up with the fruit of His Spirit, which is love, joy, peace, patience, kindness, goodness and self control.

WORSHIP

Another way to be in relationship with God is in **worship**. You were created to worship your Father in heaven. A million things can happen in your heart while you are listening to music that is focused on Him and who He is. Worship can literally change you from feeling down and sad to being filled with joy, through a song. Worship takes the focus off of ourselves and our troubles and lifts them up to Him.

When we worship Jesus and sing out of our heart, we can reach down to the deepest places in our soul and connect with His love and healing. In worship, our spirits join with His and we open our mouths and sing and we release a sound to and from heaven. That sound goes out and it can shift and change atmospheres or things around us. Worship is key to walking with God, and it is awesome.

FELLOWSHIP

God does not intend for you to be alone in your walk with Him. It is His desire that you would have friends to walk alongside you and for you to pursue Him together. It is not always easy to find the right people, but if you ask God to bring the right friends into your life He will do it. It may take some time, and this is easier for some than others, but be patient and trust and He will lead you to them, or them to you.

As we share our hearts with our friends and what we are experiencing in God, He moves among us, between us and through us. This is another way we grow and develop into His likeness and find the desires and gifts He has placed inside of us. In God, we learn so much from each other. Sharing our lives spiritually can be fun and makes the most meaningful relationships that you can have.

1 Corinthians 15:33 NIV
Do not be misled "Bad company corrupts good character."

Everyone isn't good for you, and this is also an area where boundaries for your life and heart must be set. This is another reason God tells us to guard our hearts. We may think we won't let others influence our lives, but who we expose ourselves to will influence us.

I can get along with most people, but that doesn't mean I should hang with them. Not very long ago I was hanging out with a friend that was pretty negative and always complaining about things. I really wanted to be a positive influence in her life and I tried to be, for awhile. But before long, I found myself complaining when I was around her and talking about all sorts of negative things. I realized, I wasn't rubbing off on her she was rubbing off on me! I still love her, but we don't hang out anymore.

With friends who are getting into trouble, either you need to influence them for the better, or you need to stay away because if you don't, they will bring you down.

When you follow God, He will put people in your life that need to be influenced by you. But it is never your job to change someone! However, you may be the very person that someone needs to see the truth of God. You may be the one to influence others in the best of ways. If you ask for discernment, you can know pretty fast if you need to let certain friends hang around. You may even like them a lot, but in the end, who you allow in your camp will either bring light to your life, or can lead you in the wrong direction.

Today, one of my greatest friends is Laura. She says "We should be kind to everyone, but we don't have to be friends with everyone." There is much wisdom in this. She is the most uplifting friend and we laugh together all the time. I am not afraid to be myself with her because I know she is a safe person that I can trust and she wants the best for me. I know that if I make a bad choice, she would call me out in a loving way and hold me accountable. Just being around her challenges me to be more like Jesus. God answered my prayers and brought me Laura. When God brings you a friend, there is nothing like it! If you need a good one, start asking for one! He will give you a friend, or *friends,* that are even better than you can imagine!

Proverbs 13:20 NIV
Walk with the wise and become wise, for a companion of fools suffers harm.

God's desire is that you would grow in wisdom and favor. Who you hang around has everything to do with this! The truth is, you need people to build you up and help you through every season of your life. You need friends that can stand with you in making good choices, it just makes life easier and better. You are God's chosen one, protect yourself and who you let in your heart!

THANKSGIVING

It's quite possible the greatest way to be in relationship with God is to enter His gates with **Thanksgiving**. Thank Him! Thank Him for every possible good thing you can think of, for all good things come from Him. As you begin to set your heart toward Him in gratitude, great things will happen, I promise!

Psalm 100:1-5

Lift up a great shout of joy to the Lord! Go ahead and do it - everyone, everywhere! As you serve him, be glad and worship him. Sing your way into his presence with joy! And realize what this really means - we have the privilege of worshipping the Lord, our God. We are the people of his pleasure. You can pass through his open gates with the password of praise. Come bring your thank-offering to him and affectionately bless his beautiful name! For the Lord is always good and ready to receive you. He's so loving that it will amaze you! And he is famous for his faithfulness toward all. Everyone knows our God can be trusted, for he keeps his promises to every generation.

DISCUSSION
PARENTS AND LEADERS

- Share ways you have heard from God.
- Share signs you believe God has given you.

KIDS AND GROUP

- Share ways you have heard from God.
- Share signs you believe God has given you.

FAMILY AND GROUP

- In prayer, invite God to speak to your hearts and spend quiet time with Him. Write your prayers and requests to God. A great way to start is by thanking Him for all of the good things. Trust and believe you are in His presence.
- Listen for Him to speak to you and write down what He may be saying to you. If you feel lead, share with your family or group.

13

CITIZENS OF HEAVEN

THE WORLD, THE KINGDOM AND JESUS

PARENTS AND LEADERS,

This message is a declaration of who we are in Christ. I pray it inspires and encourages you and your group or family. Be blessed!

Citizens of Heaven
The World, the Kingdom and Jesus

While we are living in this world, we are not of it. The Bible describes us as resident aliens or foreigners in this world. Those of us in Christ are just passing through. Our life on earth is temporary and compared to a mist in the wind, going by fast. In the light of eternity this life is just a blip.

We are called citizens of heaven. A citizen is an inhabitant of a city or town. We are inhabitants of heaven. God has plans and purposes for us to influence earth and make it look more like heaven.

WE ARE *FROM* HEAVEN, *BRINGING* HEAVEN, ONLY TO *RETURN* TO HEAVEN

We are called to be *love* in the world, but not to love the ways of the world. As we live out our destiny on earth, we will be transformed to be like Jesus. We will influence the world around us to look like heaven. Then we will stand before God and give an account for our lives. This will be a glorious day for those of us who have followed after Him.

WALKING IN THE SUPERNATURAL

As Citizens of Heaven, we are here to bring God's will on earth. We know God's will because God's will is on earth as it is in heaven. There is no sickness, no addiction, no brokenness in heaven. As we walk with God, and we grow in Him, we can pray for people and see miracles. We can show them a love they have never seen and they will be changed. This should be our normal Christian life.

Years ago I went to a conference in Tennessee. During a beautiful worship service the leader called a little girl and her mom to come up on stage. She was about 11 years old, and she was deformed. Her arms and legs were curved and bound, and when she took a step she would bobble up and down. It looked hard for her to walk and to get around.

The woman leading worship began to sing spontaneously over her. It was a beautiful song, and in my heart I knew it was coming straight from heaven. I walked forward. Everyone walked forward to gather in the front. We all stretched out our hands and arms and began to sing our own songs along with the music. It was the most heavenly sound I have ever heard. I felt as though we had stepped into heaven itself. I had tears rolling down my face, as I felt an overwhelming love and compassion for this little girl.

The singing went on for awhile and the little girl was just sitting in a chair beside her mom on the stage. Then the woman began to sing over the mom and the mom began to cry. The little girl stood up and naturally and slowly she began to dance like a beautiful and composed ballerina. Her arms and legs straightened out and there was nothing awkward about her. She was flowing with the heavenly music and I could see that God was healing her and that her mom was getting free, and letting go of burdens in her heart. I didn't understand it all with my mind, but in my spirit I knew what was happening. God's Kingdom had come into that room. Heaven was flowing through worship and prayer, people were being changed, healed and set free.

God's desire is that we would be His hands and feet on earth. That we would pray and sing and heaven would come, and things would change. There are times I have prayed for things and they haven't been answered the way I had hoped or believed. But God has never let me down and I know He is in all things. Believing in the supernatural is part of living as a Citizen of Heaven on earth. The Kingdom of God coming on *us and through us to change the world* is what we were born for!

THE KINGDOM

It is often said that the Kingdom of God is backwards, inside out, and upside down. How could the King of all kings come as a poor baby who slept in a stinky manger where animals ate. He could have been born in the most majestic palace of all time. How could this King not have all of the earthly riches, endless servants at his feet, and not have ruled from a big shiny throne? He could have worn a kingly crown, adorned with diamonds and jewels and He could have ordered everyone on earth to do as He pleased. Instead, He was a humble servant.

Jesus, the King of all, didn't change the world with tons of money, or from power given by man. He changed it with *love* like the world had never seen. While the religious people of His day looked down upon and condemned the poor, the sinners, the sick, Jesus chose them. Jesus healed them, He set them free. Jesus gained His followers by doing things in a totally different way than the world.

Jesus' best friends, His disciples, got to walk closely with Him. Even though He was their Master, their Teacher, the One in charge, the Messiah or Savior of the world, He did the most humble and beautiful thing.

John 13

On His last night on earth, during dinner, He got up, took off His robe, and took a towel and wrapped it around His waist. He poured water into a basin and He washed His disciples dirty feet and dried them with a towel. When He got to Peter, Peter said "I can't let you wash my dirty feet, you are my Lord!" and again he said "You will never wash my dirty feet never!"

Jesus said, "But Peter, if you don't allow me to wash your feet, then you will not be able to share life with me."

There is nothing like the love of Jesus. His ways are so different and so much higher than ours. Here, He is saying, let me, the King of all kings, the Savior of the world, serve you. I will take all your dirt, all your junk, and I will make you clean. Then we can share life together. This is the gospel of Jesus Christ. Glory to His name!

Jesus knew that Judas, who was supposed to love Him and be one of his closest friends, would betray Him. Judas got money for identifying Jesus to the people who arrested Him and who ultimately hung Him on the cross. He betrayed the Savior of the world for money. Jesus knew this was coming and He still knelt down and washed Judas' feet. How could He wash his feet in such an act of humility and love?

The world will know the followers of Jesus by the way they

love and treat others. Especially the poor the sick and even our enemies. It's a natural reaction when someone hurts you or wrongs you to want to get them back. It's a kingdom reaction to wash their feet or to love them. And it is so powerful. In this upside down kingdom of God, He will raise up those who humble themselves.

Colossians 3:12 NIV

Therefore, as God's chosen people, holy and dearly loved, clothe yourselves with compassion, kindness, humility, gentleness and patience.

Jesus said that we would be blessed when we humble ourselves, when we show mercy to others, when we are peacemakers, and when we put others first. These are not just great ideas. As citizens of heaven, there are opportunities each day to practice these things. As you journey with God, I pray that He reveals these moments to you, and you will be blessed. Being blessed from heaven is better than getting your way in the moment. Test it out and you will see.

John 14:16-17

That same night (during dinner) Jesus told His disciples that God would be giving them the Holy Spirit of Truth. He described the Holy Spirit as the One "who will be to you a Friend just like me and He will never leave you." He said "The world won't receive him because they can't see him or know him. But you will know him intimately, because he will make his home in you and will live inside you."

Citizens of heaven walk with the Holy Spirit just like Jesus walked with the disciples. The world will not understand Him, but you will.

FOLLOWING JESUS ISN'T ALWAYS EASY, BUT IT'S ALWAYS WORTH IT

Jesus was misunderstood when He was on earth. He was persecuted, accused, and eventually tortured and killed. Saying *yes* to Jesus means so many great things, but there is a cost. We live in a day where we have freedom to follow Him and proclaim His name and that is amazing! However, there will be challenges to staying true to your *yes* for Jesus.

Like foreigners or aliens, many people in the world will not understand us. Our faith will offend people. Like in the days of Jesus, our faith may offend the religious people or the ones that try to reduce God to a set of traditions and rules, just like I did. Our faith may offend people in darkness who don't want to hear the truth. Jesus said, if we are standing up for Him and doing what is right, if people say bad things about us, or persecute us, we will be blessed. He even said, if that happens we should rejoice! He said we will have a great reward in heaven!

While it can be hard to be set apart, and follow Jesus in this world, when I think about what He has done for me, I know without a doubt He is worth it. It is beyond worth living my life for Him when I will be with Him for all eternity. And many in darkness are desperately waiting for you to reveal Jesus to them.

YOU ARE THE DWELLING PLACE OF GOD

John 14:23
Jesus replied, "Loving me empowers you to obey my word. And my Father will love you so deeply that we will come to you and make you our dwelling place."

Those of us that love God, will be empowered to obey Him, and because He loves us so much He will make us His dwelling place! Are you getting this?

While Jesus was on earth he did many miraculous things. Everywhere he went he healed people. He didn't just heal people that were sick, he set people free that were bound to their sin. He partnered with His Heavenly Father and he prayed for them and they got well, or got free.

So, if God the Father, and the Son, and the Holy Spirit, are dwelling or living in us, is it possible that we can do what Jesus did? Jesus actually said, whoever believes in me will do the works I have been doing, and they will do even greater things than these. He was talking to His disciples and He was talking to us.

SALT AND LIGHT

In the upside down, inside out, and backwards kingdom of God, we are called to be salt and light. Listen to what Jesus said about us as we represent the Kingdom of God.

Matthew 5:13
"'Your lives are like salt among the people. But if you, like salt, become bland, how can your 'saltiness' be restored? Flavorless salt is good for nothing and will be thrown out and trampled on by others. Your lives light up the world. Let others see your light from a distance, for how can you hide a city that stands on a hilltop? And who would light a lamp and then hide it in an obscure place? Instead, it's placed where everyone in the house can benefit from its light. So, don't hide your light! Let it shine before others, so that the commendable things you do will shine as light upon them, and then they will give their praise to your Father in heaven."

We will be run over by the world if we are just casual or bland Christians. We are not here to just fit in and follow others. We are not called to hide or cower under pressure. We are not called to be *in your face Christians*, telling people what is wrong with them, or how they need to change their behavior. We are called to be *light*. We are called to let Him shine through us. We are called to love others the way He has loved us and let them see our good works, like praying for the lost, the hurting and the sick. Like serving others and washing their feet. Living and loving like Jesus. When they see that, they will praise God!

Being a citizen of heaven means knowing who you are. We have the greatest guidebook and instruction manual of all. The Bible. God's Word is a lamp unto our feet and a light unto our path. It is vital to our life here on earth. Reading the Bible is a powerful way to know who you are and what God is saying. So often people misrepresent God and even scripture, but when you have a relationship with the author of it all, the Bible is alive. And to have a relationship with Him, you need His word. Not only that, it's crazy good.

1 Peter 2:9

But you are a chosen people, a royal priesthood, a holy nation, God's special possession, that you may declare the praises of him who called you out of darkness into his wonderful light.

We are chosen and set apart. We are kings and queens of the most high God. We are sons and daughters and priests and saints. We are citizens of the greatest Kingdom that could ever be and we are blessed. This life is such a gift from God. We will be forever praising Him not only for who He is but for what Jesus did for us so that we could be with Him in paradise forever. We may live to be one hundred or we may live until tomorrow, we don't know. But what we do know, is that living *for* Him is worth it. He is worth it. For giving us life, for saving us, and for giving us eternity. Being a citizen of heaven means bringing light, life, hope and love to all people and all situations.

DISCUSSION
FAMILY AND GROUP

- Choose someone to read Philippians 3:18-21. Then
  break it down and discuss it.

Philippians 3:18-21 NIV

For, as I have often told you before and now tell you again
even with tears, many live as enemies of the cross of Christ.
Their destiny is destruction, their god is their stomach, and
their glory is in their shame. Their mind is set on earthly things.
But our citizenship is in heaven. And we eagerly await a Savior
from there, the Lord Jesus Christ, who, by the power that
enables him to bring everything under his control, will
transform our lowly bodies so that they will be like his glorious
body.

- Read this beautiful scripture about God's word.

Psalm 19:7

God's word is perfect in every way; how it revives our souls!
His laws lead us to truth,
and his ways change the simple into wise.
His teachings make us joyful and radiate his light;
his precepts are so pure!
His commands, how they challenge us
to keep close to his heart!
The revelation-light of his work makes
my spirit shine radiant.
Every one of the Lord's commands is right;
following them brings cheer.
Nothing he says ever needs to be changed.

The rarest treasures of life are found in his truth.
That's why I prize God's word like others
prize the finest gold.
Nothing brings the soul such sweetness
as seeking his living words.
For they warn us, his servants, and keep us from
following the wicked way, giving a lifetime guarantee:
great success to ever obedient soul!
Without revelation-light,
how would I ever detect the waywardness of my heart?
Lord, forgive my hidden flaws whenever you find them.
Keep cleansing me, God, and keep me from my secret,
selfish sins; may then never rule over me!
Only then will I be free from fault
and remain innocent of rebellion.
So may the words of my mouth, my meditation-thoughts,
and every moment of my heart be always pure and pleasing,
acceptable before your eyes, my only Redeemer,
my Protector-God.

- Discuss favorite books or verses that you have in the Bible.
- Discuss how and when you like to read the Bible and give direction and encouragement to your child or group about good ways to engage in scripture.

PRAYER

Thank You God for choosing us and setting us apart in this dark world. Thank You God for sending Jesus so that we could be citizens of the greatest kingdom there ever will be. Thank You for providing every-thing we need to be successful in this life as we follow You. Thank You for inviting us to be the light of the world and for dwelling in us and living through us. Thank You Jesus for being the perfect example of love and humility. Help us to be transformed to be like You in all that we do. Help us to see and to know our purpose here on earth. Thank You for giving us the Bible. Give us wisdom and understanding to know Your Word. Thank You that it is a joy to learn about where we come from, where we belong, and where we are going. In Jesus name, Amen.

14

A CROWN OF BEAUTY

REDEMPTION, PURPOSE AND ETERNITY

PARENTS AND LEADERS,

Thank you for taking this journey and for sharing it with your children, class or small group. I know there is so much more. I pray not one person would misunderstand the love, grace or truth of our Lord Jesus Christ. I pray none of this sounds preachy or self righteous, everything good in me comes from Him, and He has turned all of my troubles into triumphs and I am a work in progress! Thank you most of all for engaging with your children and being willing to take some hard topics and face them head on. Let's flip the switch on the enemy and believe for the best years to come for our preteens and teens. I hope God has blessed you richly and awakened you and your children to Him, in new and amazing ways. God Bless!

A Crown of Beauty
Redemption, Purpose and Eternity

Romans 8:37-39

Yet even in the midst of all these things, we triumph over them all, for God has made us to be more than conquerors, and his demonstrated love is our glorious victory over everything! So now I live with the confidence that there is nothing in the universe with the power to separate us from God's love. I'm convinced that his love will triumph over death, life's troubles, fallen angels, or dark rulers in the heavens. There is nothing in our present or future circumstances that can weaken his love. There is no power above us or beneath us- no power that could ever be found in the universe that can distance us from God's passionate love, which is lavished upon us through our Lord Jesus, the Anointed One!

I can tell you all about the choices you will face. I can beg and plead with you to make the right ones. In your heart you know right from wrong. That isn't always enough. There is a battle for your life. Not just for you to go to heaven someday. The enemy doesn't want you to know who you are. He doesn't want you to know that you belong, that you are loved. As you give your heart to Jesus and allow Him to know all of you, you will encounter His love. When you do that, you will be empowered to make choices that will lead you down the path He has laid for you. You will not only be living your best life, you will be changing the world around you.

He has laid a path for you that brings freedom for you to be who He created you to be, no matter what the world is saying. The message the world sends is that you aren't enough, or you are too much. If you allow the influence of the world to be louder than your Heavenly Father's voice, you may end up in battles you weren't meant to face. You will make mistakes. You will make wrong choices. It will never change the way God feels about you. No matter what happens, He can always pick you up, bring you back, redeem and restore you. His desire is that you stick with Him.

Jesus said in this world you will have trouble but don't worry, because He has overcome the world. Jesus has already overcome every single struggle you will face. If you are going through a hard time or you feel like you are in the fire, God is near. His word tells us He draws near to those with broken hearts. If your heart is troubled or you are hurting, He is extra near to you, just reach out to Him.

Whatever issues you face in your life, God has you. The Holy Spirit, your inside BFF, is with you. As you set your mind on Him, cast your cares on Him, and allow Him to guide you through temptations and desires, you will be transformed into His likeness.

Once I woke up to the life God had for me, I saw Him in everything! I saw signs and wonders and miracles happening. I began to interact with the God of all things and I will never go back to a life without Him.

God has put passion and desires in my heart to speak life and truth over others. He has called me to share His love and to set the captives free. And that it what He is calling you to do!

I love to encourage others and build them up by sharing what I believe He says about them. I have learned that this is one of my great purposes in life. When God gives me the opportunity to do that, I feel more alive and full of excitement and joy. Sometimes I can just feel His heart for someone and it blesses me to be able to share it. I want everyone to wake up to the gifts God has put inside them.

On an ordinary day, I was walking down the street listening to worship music and I just knew I was in the presence of God. There was so much grace and love and peace. In my path was a guy who looked pretty rough. He may have been on drugs or under the influence of something, you could just tell he was in a bad place. God showed me His heart for this guy. Then my heart was overwhelmed with love, grace and mercy for him. I just wanted to bless him and share God's love for him. I didn't want to go up to him and tell him all of the things I thought he was doing wrong and all the things he needed to do, I think he probably knew all of that. I just wanted to share the mercy and love God gave me with him, because that's what changed me. That's what will change the world.

Moments like these give meaning and value and eternal purpose to my life. Following Jesus has filled a void only He could fill. Wherever I am, **Jesus goes before me, walks beside me and flows through me.** When I face opposition or enemies, He is my defender. I can be in the toughest of times and He gives me what I need and then some. He can fill me with the greatest joy on the saddest or hardest of days. In Him, I am loved beyond my wildest dreams and so are you.

VICTORY OVER THE GRAVE

My favorite person ever was my brother. If I could only explain how great he was. Of any person I have ever known, he reminded me of Jesus. He had a great love and compassion for others and he saw God in most everything.

It was nice and easy for me when he was around because when I stuck close to him, I knew I would be ok. My brother would always protect me. If anyone ever said something hurtful to me, he would defend me. When I didn't know the right things to say or how to act, I could just do what he did. I liked the same music he liked and I generally had the same friends he had. Basically, I followed in his footsteps and I modeled myself after him.

The love I felt from my brother made me feel safe. Whenever I was around him I was comfortable and free. I knew that he loved and accepted me no matter what. He made me laugh a lot! He was really funny. He was smart too. I felt if it was a choice he was making, it was ok for me to make.

My brother had a way of making everyone feel loved and special. It wasn't an act, it was just who he was. He was a guy that was cool, but wasn't afraid to have emotions and feelings and compassion. He would treat the person that was a nobody the same, if not better, than he would treat a famous person. He wasn't concerned with being a big shot, he was humble and kind, and he lived in the moment and made it count.

People were drawn to him because of the way he made them feel. Being around him meant you felt loved, accepted, understood and maybe sometimes closer to God.

My brother wasn't perfect. He made some bad decisions, and so did I. But as far back as I can remember he was seeking Jesus. I learned so much from him.

When I got the news that my brother died, everything I knew came crashing down in one moment. The foundation that I built my life on collapsed. My identity, or who I thought I was, was wrapped up in everything Dylan.

When they told me he was gone, all I could say over and over was, not my brother, not my brother, not my brother. Of all people to lose, the one I loved the most. The very thought of him suffering or hurting and dying, was too much to bear.

If someone had offered me all of the beauty in the world, to give me the perfect body and hair and face, it wouldn't have made me feel better. If someone had offered to give me all of the popularity or to make me a movie star and to be the most famous person on the planet, it wouldn't have even mattered. If I was offered one billion dollars so I could have the best of everything, it wouldn't have taken an ounce of the pain out of my heart. It wouldn't bring him back.

When he died, I felt I was left with nothing. I got on my knees and cried out to God for help and love overwhelmed me. Love broke down every wall that was surrounding my heart. Everything I had tried to hide from God was laid bare before Him. I gave up running, hiding, and pretending. I surrendered my guilt and shame and insecurity. I had nothing to give him but my brokenness and my pain.

The craziest thing is that is exactly what He wanted from me. Not only did He lift the heavy sorrow and sadness, but He filled me. Something that was impossible, supernatural, and miraculous happened. Something that not all of the worldly beauty, fame or fortune could buy, He provided.

He took my fear of living without my brother and He gave me peace that doesn't even make sense. When I lost *what I felt was everything to me*, He showed me that actually, *He had everything I needed,* and He would never leave me or let me down. Even though I had nothing to offer Him but my brokenness, He told me that was enough. *I was enough.*

He took my guilt and shame, and He covered it with love that is beyond what we can imagine. **I saw that His love was what I was made for.** He took my insecurities about myself and He told me I was beautiful. When God tells you something, you just believe it!

It was His love, that took my brother's failures and sins to the cross. Jesus took them on himself, so that my brother could go to Heaven. In Heaven, my brother is free. He isn't in the clouds somewhere, he is with Jesus on streets paved with gold. There is a river there, and it flows from the throne of God. That's where my brother is!

Oh, how I still miss him. There are so many times I wish he was here. But God always gives me signs of His promise that one day we'll be together forever and ever.

When I worship, often I feel I am standing next to my brother at the feet of Jesus. It is the most beautiful thing and it's real. Someday soon, I will be there with him, and for 10,000 years we will worship God in fullness together, and that will only be the beginning.

My brother was everything to me, but when I lost him, I realized I was putting him in a spot he didn't belong. Following *Dylan* was never going to be enough. God made me unique, and while Dylan was amazing, I am different than him. Losing Dylan was the hardest thing I had faced, but it was when I fully surrendered my life to God. It was when I began to truly live.

I gave up trying to follow the rules to get to God. I gave up trying to earn a place with Him. I let go of being good enough and doing the right things. I just was. He took me in and He loved me.

For the first time I fully knew I was seen and loved completely and that I belonged. I had been searching for 27 years for that. Nothing I had done to try to fill that void in my life could touch the truth of who God is for me and how He feels about me. Nothing I learned about right and wrong had the power to change me. But one moment in His presence and I will never be the same.

The truth is, He was always there, pursuing me, chasing me, protecting me and loving me. I just didn't feel worthy to respond. But because of Jesus, I am. And because of Jesus you are too. He will never ever stop pursuing you and even when you accept His love...*He has more.*

The truth is, He is the way, the truth and the life. This life is not about us, it's about *Him*. God designed you and I to live our lives for Jesus. God designed us to live forever because in Him we will. God made us for something so much bigger and better than this world, or just religious duty, and our lives on earth are an opportunity to see His power flow through us. There are sick, broken and hurting people out there. They are waiting to be set free, healed and delivered from darkness. They need the very thing God has put inside you. You may go through some hard times, but everything that the enemy has stolen from your life, God will restore, and then some! As you walk out your purpose and destiny with Him, you will be transformed and you will bring Heaven to earth.

I leave you with lyrics from a song I love called, *Walking Resurrection,* by Curt Vernon:

"You sing over me
　　the song that you sing is love and rest and peace

you're in love with me
and I resurrect the moment I receive

I'm like a walking resurrection
I'm on this earth with heaven's feet
and all of this love you've lavished on me
It grew contagious now it's flowing out of me

I am now quite sure
if I so much as ask you'd give me more
I have grown convinced
that all that you've done before you'll do again

I'm like a walking resurrection
stones are rolling away everywhere I go
for those who doubt you're even out there
I know once they meet me they'll know for sure

I'm like a walking resurrection
Stones are rolling away everywhere I go
For those who doubt you're even out there
I know once they meet me they'll know for sure
I know once they meet me they'll know for sure.

No one is going to leave this place captive
no one is going to leave this place in chains
because the blood that you spilled for me
left freedom running through my veins
no one is going to leave this place captive
no one is going to leave this place in chains
because the blood that you spilled for me
left freedom running through my veins
left freedom running through my veins

I wanna hear you singing over me
    wanna hear you singing over me
    it's what my heart craves, what it means
    just to hear you singing over me

I'm like a walking resurrection
    heaven and earth are growing hard to tell apart
    see I believe the kingdom of power
    is about to wage a war on the kingdom of talk

I said I believe that the kingdom of power is about to wage a war on the kingdom of talk"

DISCUSSION
FAMILY AND GROUP

- Open discussion, ministry time and prayer.

Isaiah 61:1-11 NIV

The Spirit of the Sovereign Lord is on me, because the Lord has anointed me to proclaim the good news to the poor.

He has sent me to bind up the brokenhearted, to proclaim freedom for the captives and release from darkness for the prisoners, to proclaim the year of the Lord's favor and the day of vengeance of our God, to comfort all who mourn, and provide for those who grieve in Zion- to bestow on them a crown of beauty instead of ashes, the oil of joy instead of mourning, and a garment of praise instead of a spirit of despair.

They will be called oaks of righteousness, a planting of the Lord for the display of his splendor.

They will rebuild the ancient ruins and restore the places long devastated; they will renew the ruined cities that have been devastated for generations.

Strangers will shepherd your flocks; foreigners will work your fields and vineyards.

And you will be called priests of the Lord, you will be named ministers of our God.

You will feed on the wealth of nations, and in their riches you will boast.

Instead of your shame you will receive a double portion, and instead of disgrace you will rejoice in your inheritance. And so you will inherit a double portion in your land, and everlasting joy will be yours.

"For I, the Lord, love justice; I hate robbery and wrongdoing. In my faithfulness I will reward my people and make an everlasting covenant with them.

Their descendants will be known among the nations and their offspring among the people.

All who see them will acknowledge that they are a people the Lord has blessed."

I delight greatly in the Lord; my soul rejoices in my God.

For he has clothed me with garments of salvation and arrayed me in a robe of his righteousness, as a bridegroom adorns his head like a priest, and as a bride adorns herself with her jewels.

For the soil makes the sprout come up and a garden causes seeds to grow so the Sovereign Lord will make righteousness and praise spring up before all nations.

Isaiah 60:1-5 NIV

Arise, shine, for your light has come, and the glory of the LORD rises upon you.

See, darkness covers the earth and thick darkness is over the people, but the Lord rises upon you and his glory appears over you.

Nations will come to your light, and kings to the brightness of your dawn.

"Lift up your eyes and look about you: All assemble and come to you; your sons come from afar, and your daughters are carried on the hip.

Then you will look and be radiant, your heart will throb and swell with joy; the wealth on the seas will be brought to you, to you the riches of the nations will come.

ABOUT THE AUTHOR

Allison Michel has a gift to talk practically with parents and youth about difficult subjects. She has a passion to see families walking in deeper connection with each other and with God. She uses her experience in overcoming failures, trials and tragedy to shed light on temptations and struggles by depending on the Holy Spirit. Allison is a wife and mother who seeks the Lord and loves to share Him with others.

DISCOVER MORE ONLINE:

THE**NOBLE**CITY.COM